MAKING MEANING

GCSE ENGLISH FOR SCHOOLS

Judith Baxter

CAMBRIDGE UNIVERSITY PRESS
Cambridge
New York   Port Chester
Melbourne   Sydney

Published by the Press Syndicate of the University of Cambridge
The Pitt Building, Trumpington Street, Cambridge CB2 1RP
40 West 20th Street, New York, NY 10011, USA
10 Stamford Road, Oakleigh, Melbourne 3166, Australia

© Cambridge University Press 1991

First published 1991
Printed in Hong Kong by Wing King Tong

British Library Cataloguing in Publication Data
Baxter, Judith
Making meaning: an English course for keystage 4.
1. English language. Usage
I. Title
428

ISBN 0-521-37688-2

Produced by Zoë Books Limited
15 Worthy Lane, Winchester
Hampshire SO23 7AB England

Designed by John Douet
Artwork by Tony Kenyon
Picture research by Jennifer Johnson and Janet Moore

NOTICE TO TEACHERS

The contents of this book are in the copyright of Cambridge University
Press. Unauthorised copying of any of the pages is
not only illegal but also goes against the interests of the author.

For authorised copying please check that your school has a licence
(through the Local Education Authority) from the Copyright Licensing Agency
which enables you to copy small parts of the text in limited numbers.

Contents

To the Teacher	6

PART ONE: WAYS OF COMMUNICATING — 7

1 · Telling my own story — 8
Nikki-Rosa by Nikki Giovanni	10
Digging by Seamus Heaney	11
Moonwalk by Michael Jackson	12
A Life in the Day of Debra McArthur from *The Sunday Times Magazine*	15

2 · Narrating — 20
Sukhinder's Grandmother's Story	22
Poor but Honest Anon	23
The Werewolf by Angela Carter	24
Abseil Escape for 59 in Skyride Hell from *Today*	27

3 · Describing people — 34
The Welcome Table by Alice Walker	36

4 · Describing places — 44
Midsummer, Tobago by Derek Walcott	44
South Side by James Smith	48
The Deserted House by Virginia Woolf	49
Case study: *The estate agency*	50

5 · Living English — 54
Visiting the Doctor by M. and J. Hobbs	56
Uncle George by Barbara Hoy	58
Favourite Shade by Liz Lochhead	60
The Dropout by Tom Leonard	60
De Youths by Nefertiti Gayle	61
A Collier's Wife by D. H. Lawrence	62
The Oxford Voice by D. H. Lawrence	63

6 · Using dialogue — 68
Keeping the Lines of Communication Open by Posy Simmonds	70
Teenagerspeak by Keith Ray	71
A Netful of Holes devised for the Second Wave Festival	72
Formica by Jonathan Steffan	74

7 · Expressing my thoughts — 80
My thoughts by Sarah Gristwood	80
"I Have a Dream" by Martin Luther King	82
Caged Bird by Maya Angelou	84
Mountains o' Things by Tracy Chapman	85

8 · Instructing — 90
Instructions for Making a Water-lily	93
Surviving Shyness by Dr John Nicholson	94
Collecting Aluminium Drinks Cans a leaflet from The Aluminium Can Recycling Association	97

9 · Complaining — 102
Case study: *Holiday complaint*	104
Holiday Upset from *Which?*	109

10 · Reporting — 112
Didcot Railway Centre News a press release from the Great Western Society	114
The show will go on from the *Daily Mail*	115
Hampstead Shooting Case from the *Illustrated Mail*	116
The Wrecking of a Northampton Music Hall from the *Illustrated Mail*	117
The Irish Triangle an ITV news item	118
Young Britain is growing up in a most alarming way from *The Sunday Times*	120

11 · Discussing **126**

How important is television really? a transcript
from *Wogan*   128
Letters from the *Guardian*   130
The television debate by Pauline Leonard   131

12 · Persuading **138**

The Passionate Shepherd to His Love by
Christopher Marlowe   140
Flash Gordon to Dale Arden by a student   141
Case study: *Young people in need*   148

13 · Arguing **152**

Should this rabbit be used in experiments?   154
Myths about Independent Schools from an ISIS
leaflet   156
Private education is wrong by Hélène Smith   157
Case study: *Argue your case!*   160

14 · Campaigning **164**

Case study: *Local campaign*   171

PART TWO: WAYS OF WORKING **175**

Keeping a study log   176
Reading and responding   177
The writing process   179
Interviewing   194
Role play   197
Formal letters   199
Leaflets   201
Sound scripts   203
Storyboards   204
Television or film scripts   205
Direct speech   206
Play scripts   207
Designing a poster   208

Acknowledgements

The author and publishers wish to thank the following who have kindly granted permission for the use of copyright material:

W.H. Allen & Co. for an extract from *Extremely Serious Guide to Parenthood* by Keith Ray (1986).
Aluminium Can Recycling Association for extracts from their leaflet.
Bernard Ashley for extracts from the draft manuscript of his book *Janey* published by Penguin Books (1987).
B.T. Batsford Ltd. for a menu and drawing from *Cockney Dialect and Slang* by Peter Wright.
British Broadcasting Corporation for an extract from the transcript of a discussion on the WOGAN programme, reproduced by permission of Mary Whitehouse, Ludovic Kennedy, Andrew Neil, and Terry Wogan.
Jane Carlisle for her letter published in *The Guardian*, January 11, 1989.
Consumers' Association for extracts from *Which? At Your Service*, October, 1988, and *Which?* February, 1988.
The Controller of HMSO for a Department of Transport poster, 'A Sobering Thought' (1986).
EMI Songs Limited/International Music Publications for 'Mountain o' Things' by Tracy Chapman from the record album *Tracy Chapman*. © 1988 April Music Inc./Purple Rabbit Music, USA. EMI Songs Ltd., London.
English & Media Centre (formerly the ILEA English Centre) for the poem 'South Side' by James Smith from *City Lines*.
Faber and Faber Ltd. for the poems 'Midsummer, Tobago' from *Collected Poems* by Derek Walcott, and 'Digging' from *Death of a Naturalist* by Seamus Heaney.
Nefertiti Gayle for her poem 'De Youths' from *Watchers and Seekers* published by The Women's Press Ltd.
Gemini News Service for the article 'Tainted Love' by Elaine Shein.
Victor Gollancz Ltd. for the story 'The Werewolf' from *The Bloody Chamber* by Angela Carter.
Great Western Society Ltd. for the Didcot Railway Centre Press Release, July 1989.
William Heinemann Ltd. for an extract from *Moonwalk* by Michael Jackson. © 1988 by Michael Jackson.
David Higham Associates Ltd. on behalf of Alice Walker for the story 'The Welcome Table' from *In Love and in Trouble* published by The Women's Press (1984).
Anna Home for her letter published in *The Guardian*, January 11, 1989.
Horizon Holidays Ltd. for extracts from their brochure.
Barbara Hoy for her poem 'Uncle George' from *Cockney Dialect and Slang*, edited by Peter Wright, published by B.T. Batsford Ltd.
Independent Schools Information Service for their fact card 'Myths about Independent Schools' (1987).
Tom Leonard for his poem 'The Dropout' from *Intimate Voices: Selected Work 1965-1983* published by the Galloping Dog Press.
London Weekend Television for the transcript of the programme EYEWITNESS, January 15, 1989.
National Anti-Vivisection Society for the article 'Should this Rabbit be used in Experiments? – No' by Jan Creamer, General Secretary.
The National Association for the Teaching of English for the story 'Sukhinder's Grandmother's Story' from the article 'The Development of Oral Storytelling' by Pat Montgomery and Rachel Robinson in *English in Education*, Summer 1989.
National Council of YMCAs for an Appeals Letter.
Dr. John Nicholson for the extract 'Surviving Shyness' published in *Issues*. Summer 1989, by Barclays Bank PLC, and from *The Good Interview Guide* (1989) published by Rosters Ltd.
Penguin Books Ltd. for 'My Thoughts' by Sara Gristwood from *Penguin English Project Stage Two: Openings*, edited by Alex McLeod (1972).
Peters Fraser & Dunlop Group Ltd. on behalf of Posy Simmonds for the cartoon 'Keeping the Lines of Communication Open' published in *The Guardian*, May 10, 1988.
Polygon for the poem 'Favourite Shade' from *True Confessions and New Clichés* by Liz Lochhead.
Random Century Ltd. on behalf of the Executors of the Virginia Woolf Estate for an extract from *To the Lighthouse* published by The Hogarth Press.
Research Defence Society for the article 'Should this Rabbit be used in Experiments? – Yes' by Margaret Franklin and Mark Matfield.
Rachel Robinson and Pat Montgomery for the story 'Sukhinder's Grandmother's Story' from the article 'The Development of Oral Storytelling' in *English in Education*, Summer 1989, the journal of the National Association for the Teaching of English.
Robson Books Ltd. for an extract from *The Words and Works of Martin Luther King, Jnr.* by Coretta Scott King.
Shelter (National Campaign for the Homeless) for publicity material.
Hélène Smith for an article 'Private Education is Wrong'.
Solo Syndication and Literary Agency Ltd. on behalf of Baz Bamigboye for the article 'The Show will go on' published in the *Daily Mail*, March 1989.
Times Newspapers Limited for the article 'A Day in the life of Debra McArthur', photograph by Tim O'Sullivan, in *The Sunday Times Magazine*, March 27, 1988; the cartoon 'You Say Tomahto' by Michael Heath, in *The Sunday Times*, January 15, 1989, and the article by Greg Hadfield and Tim Rayment 'Young Britain is growing up in a most alarming way' in *The Sunday Times*, November 13, 1988. Statistics in the article were from *Young People in 1988* by John Balding of HEA Schools Health Education Unit, University of Exeter, and reproduced by permission.
TODAY Newspaper for the article 'Abseil escape for 59 in sky ride hell' by Alan Qualtrough and Steve McKinlay, March 25, 1989.
Virago Press Limited for the poem 'Caged Bird' by Maya Angelou.
Victor Watson and signatories for their letter published in *The Guardian*, January 11, 1989.
Ward Lock Educational, East Grinstead, for the poem 'Nikki-Rosa' by Nikki Giovanni from *Into Poetry* by Richard Andrews (1983).
Darrell Warner for the cover artwork on *Janey* by Bernard Ashley, first published in Puffin, 1986.
The Women's Press for 'A Netful of Holes' by Second Wave Young Women Playwrights from *Dead Proud* (1987).

Every effort has been made to trace all the copyright holders but if any have been inadvertently overlooked the publishers will be pleased to make the necessary arrangement at the first opportunity.

The author and publishers would also like to thank the following for permission to reproduce photographs:
p7 the Tate Gallery, London; p8 (x3) Sally & Richard Greenhill; p11 J Allan Cash Photo Library; p13 David Redfern/Redferns; p15 Tim O'Sullivan/Times Newspapers Ltd; p20 Douglas Dickins Photo Library; p23 The Fitzwilliam Museum, Cambridge; p24 Hamburger Kunsthalle; p26 Empics; (inset) News Team; p30 Pomme Clayton/The Company of Storytellers; p38 Robert Harding Picture Library; p44 Barnaby's Picture Library; p46 J Allan Cash Picture Library; p47 Trevor Hill; p48 P D Barkshire/Barnaby's Picture Library; p52 (x3) Sally & Richard Greenhill; p58 Clive Sawyer/ZEFA; p62 ZEFA; p63 Telegraph Colour Library; p68 Phil Dixon/Newport Survey; p73 Val Wilmer/Format; p83 Topham Picture Source; p84 J Allan Cash Photo Library; p85 Henrietta E Smith/Redferns; p90 Peter J Millard/ICI/Cunningham Wain; p106 Barnaby's Picture Library; p107 (x2) J Allan Cash Photo Library; p115 Solo Syndication; p119 G Mabbs/ZEFA; p121 Times Newspapers Ltd; p125 Philips Consumer Electronics; p126 Trevor Hill; p138 (x5) Next; p140 Staatliche Kunstsammlungen, Dresden; p141 The Kobal Collection; p143 National Council of YMCAs; p144 National Council of YMCAs; p146 Mark Edwards/Shelter; p147 Rachel Morton/Shelter; 152 Barry Waddams; p154/155 Trevor Hill; p158 Sally & Richard Greenhill; p164 Jenny Matthews/Format; p175 Kunstmuseum, Bern.

To the Teacher

Aims of the book

This book is intended for Key Stage 4 students (15/16 year olds) who are following a course in English such as GCSE. It responds fully to the requirements for English in the National Curriculum, and also aims to take account of the differing needs of examining groups around the country.

MAKING MEANING intends principally to encourage students to explore and experiment widely with language. With the work of LINC (Language in the National Curriculum) in mind, it has a more investigative approach to language than many English coursebooks. It asks students to reflect more consciously on language as a tool of thought and as a medium of self-expression. The book guides students towards more precisely defined and crafted English work through activities designed to initiate discussion and experimentation with language.

How the book is organised

MAKING MEANING has two main parts. The first, *Ways of Communicating* contains a series of chapters, each about a particular way of using language, and following a similar pattern. The *Starters* are light, largely oral, introductory activities, which invite students to have fun with language. These are followed by the reading material, which provides real examples of language, and usually, complete texts. The *Activities* offer a choice of more demanding areas of study, both oral and written. The *Techniques* section accompanies and complements the activities, offering a structured insight into a way of using language.

The second part of the book, *Ways of Working*, is a reference section offering guidance on the process of language work from idea generation and drafting, through to the final presentation of a piece of coursework. Many of the chapters in *Ways of Communicating* are cross-referenced with *Ways of Working*. So, a student writing a magazine article about 'A Life in the Day of . . .' on p.15, is directed to look at the advice on interviewing techniques on pp.194-196.

How to use this book

The book is intended to be used flexibly as a learning resource, rather than as a formal coursebook to be followed from start to finish. Each chapter can be studied independently; in relation to two or three other chapters; or as part of an overall programme of study. The book encourages students to take a role in shaping their own learning. They should be able to read through any section on their own, with a partner, or in groups. They may then consider the choices of activities relating to the reading material, and make decisions about the type of work they wish to do.

The methodology of the book encourages students to realise their own importance in the dynamic process of reading, interpreting, criticising and creating language – as makers of meaning.

Judith Baxter

Part One

WAYS OF COMMUNICATING

1 · Telling my own story

Memory triggers

A famous French writer, Marcel Proust, began writing about his memories after he was reminded of his childhood by the taste of a small cake called a 'madeleine'. This taste was the trigger which brought back memories of the times when he had tea with his aunt. In pairs, think about whether you have a trigger that brings back memories of your childhood. For example:

- a piece of music,
- a film or TV programme,
- a certain drink or food,
- a particular smell, such as the sea or floor polish,
- an item of clothing,
- something you see at a relative's house.

Snapshots of the past

Bring into class some items from your childhood which trigger memories for you – for example, two or three photographs taken at different moments in your childhood; an old toy, game or piece of clothing. In pairs, try to recall all the associations you have with these belongings – people, places, incidents.

Then work with another pair, and take turns to tell the story behind one particular photograph or belonging. If you can, explain its significance for your life then and now.

'Staging' your past

In groups, think about how you might 'stage' the story behind a photograph or belonging. Choosing the story of one person from your group, use *one* of these approaches:

> a) **A tableau:** produce a *still* image of the story (perhaps based on a photograph). You should each take the role of a person or an object in the story. Use facial expressions, gestures, body posture and spacing between people to represent what happened, the relationships between people and so on.
>
> b) **A mime:** act out the story using the same approaches as (a), but in motion.
>
> Perform your tableau or mime before members of your class. Ask them to guess what is going on and perhaps to suggest a title.

Writers may tell stories about their childhood and home backgrounds in a poem:

Nikki-Rosa

childhood rememberances are always a drag
if you're Black
you always remember things like living in Woodlawn
with no inside toilet
and if you become famous or something
they never talk about how happy you were to have your mother
all to yourself and
how good the water felt when you got your bath from one of those
big tubs that folk in chicago barbecue in
and somehow when you talk about home
it never gets across how much you
understood their feelings
as the whole family attended meetings about Hollydale
and even though you remember
your biographers never understand
your father's pain as he sells his stock
and another dream goes
and though you're poor it isn't poverty that
concerns you
and though they fought a lot
it isn't your father's drinking that makes any difference
but only that everybody is together and you
and your sister have happy birthdays and very good christmasses
and I really hope no white person ever has cause to write about me
because they never understand Black love is Black wealth and they'll
probably talk about my hard childhood and never understand that
all the while I was quite happy

Nikki Giovanni

Digging

Between my finger and my thumb
The squat pen rests; snug as a gun.

Under my window, a clean rasping sound
When the spade sinks into gravelly ground:
My father, digging. I look down.

Till his straining rump among the flowerbeds
Bends low, comes up twenty years away
Stooping in rhythm through potato drills
Where he was digging.

The coarse boot nestled on the lug, the shaft
Against the inside knee was levered firmly.
He rooted out tall tops, buried the bright edge deep
To scatter new potatoes that we picked
Loving their cool hardness in our hands.

By God, the old man could handle a spade.
Just like his old man.

My grandfather cut more turf in a day
Than any other man on Toner's bog.
Once I carried him milk in a bottle
Corked sloppily with paper. He straightened up
To drink it, then fell to right away
Nicking and slicing neatly, heaving sods
Over his shoulder, going down and down
For the good turf. Digging.

The cold smell of potato mould, the squelch and slap
Of soggy peat, the curt cuts of an edge
Through living roots awaken in my head.
But I've no spade to follow men like them.

Between my finger and my thumb
The squat pen rests.
I'll dig with it.

Seamus Heaney

Michael Jackson wrote about his childhood and home background in an autobiography, written at the age of twenty-nine.

Moonwalk

I've always wanted to be able to tell stories, you know, stories that came from my soul. I'd like to sit by a fire and tell people stories – make them see pictures, make them cry and laugh, take them *anywhere* emotionally with something as deceptively simple as words. I'd like to tell tales to move their souls and transform them. I've always wanted to be able to do that. Imagine how the great writers must feel, knowing they have that power. I sometimes feel I *could* do it. It's something I'd like to develop. In a way, songwriting uses the same skills, creates the emotional highs and lows, but the story is a sketch. It's quicksilver. There are very few books written on the art of storytelling, how to grip listeners, how to get a group of people together and amuse them. No costumes, no makeup, no nothing, just you and your voice, and your powerful ability to take them anywhere, to transform their lives, if only for minutes.

As I begin to tell my story, I want to repeat what I usually say to people when they ask me about my earliest days with the Jackson 5: I was so little when we began to work on our music that I really don't remember much about it. Most people have the luxury of careers that start when they're old enough to know exactly what they're doing and why, but, of course, that wasn't true of me. They remember everything that happened to them, but I was only five years old. When you're a show business child, you really don't have the maturity to understand a great deal of what is going on around you. People make a lot of decisions concerning your life when you're out of the room. So here's what I remember. I remember singing at the top of my voice and dancing with real joy and working too hard for a child. Of course, there are many details I don't remember at all. I do remember the Jackson 5 really taking off when I was only eight or nine.

I was born in Gary, Indiana, on a late summer night in 1958, the seventh of my parents' nine children. My father, Joe Jackson, was born in Arkansas, and in 1949 he married my mother, Katherine Scruse, whose people came from Alabama. My sister Maureen was born the following year and had the tough job of being the oldest. Jackie, Tito, Jermaine, LaToya, and Marlon were all next in line. Randy and Janet came after me.

A part of my earliest memories is my father's job working in the steel mill. It was tough, mind-numbing work and he played

The Jackson Five

music for escape. At the same time, my mother was working in a department store. Because of my father, and because of my mother's own love of music, we heard it all the time at home. My father and his brother had a group called the Falcons who were the local R&B band. My father played the guitar, as did his brother. They would do some of the great early rock 'n' roll and blues songs by Chuck Berry, Little Richard, Otis Redding, you name it. All those styles were amazing and each had an influence on Joe and on us, although we were too young to know it at the time. The Falcons practiced in the living room of our house in Gary, so I was raised on R&B. Since we were nine kids and my father's brother had eight of his own, our combined numbers made for a huge family. Music was what we did for entertainment and those times helped keep us together and kind of encouraged my father to be a family-oriented man. The Jackson 5 were born out of this tradition – we later became the Jacksons – and because of this training and musical tradition, I moved out on my own and established a sound that is mine.

I remember my childhood as mostly work, even though I *loved* to sing. I wasn't *forced* into this business by stage parents the way Judy Garland was. I did it because I enjoyed it and because it was as natural to me as drawing a breath and exhaling it. I did it because I was *compelled* to do it, not by parents or family, but by my own inner life in the world of music.

There were times, let me make that clear, when I'd come home from school and I'd only have time to put my books down and get ready for the studio. Once there, I'd sing until late at night, until it was past my bedtime, really. There was a park across the street from the Motown studio, and I can remember looking at those kids playing games. I'd just stare at them in wonder – I couldn't imagine such freedom, such a carefree life – and wish more than anything that I had that kind of freedom, that I could walk away and be like them. So there were sad moments in my childhood. It's true for any child star. Elizabeth Taylor told me she felt the same way. When you're young and you're working, the world can seem awfully unfair. I wasn't forced to be little Michael the lead singer – I did it and I loved it – but it was hard work. If we were doing an album, for example, we'd go off to the studio after school and I might or might not get a snack. Sometimes there just wasn't time. I'd come home, exhausted, and it'd be eleven or twelve and past time to go to bed.

So I very much identify with anyone who worked as a child. I know how they struggled, I know what they sacrificed. I also know what they learned. I've learned that it becomes more of a challenge as one gets older. I feel old for some reason. I really feel like an old soul, someone who's seen a lot and experienced a lot. Because of all the years I've clocked in, it's hard for me to accept that I am only twenty-nine. I've been in the business for twenty-four years. Sometimes I feel like I should be near the end of my life, turning eighty, with people patting me on the back. That's what comes from starting so young.

Michael Jackson from *Moonwalk*

Debra McArthur describes her life as a schoolgirl. Photograph by Tim O'Sullivan

A LIFE IN THE DAY OF
Debra McArthur

"At roughly 7.30am my radio alarm buzzes. As it is actually on my bed it literally blasts me into awareness of the morning. This is due to the loudness I need to wake me. I lie for a while deciding whether to brave the bitter cold of the surrounding room or stay in bed and pretend to be fatally ill. This trick doesn't usually work, but I try anyway. My mother never believes me. This could be due to either of two factors. Either I am a very poor actress or my mother dismisses my mysterious illness as a regular occurrence.

After the rejection I clamber out of bed clad only in a T-shirt and shorts. By this time it is 8am – the time I used to leave the house for school. I have now convinced my father that it would benefit my health and welfare to receive another hour in bed and be taken to school at 8.40am by car. He agreed, but this, to my dismay, has resulted in the immense amount of favours I now seem to owe him. I don't argue – I value sleep too much.

As I work on a Saturday (and every other Thursday night) at Geordie Jeans, I only have a lie-in on Sundays – and what a lie-in. I have my Sunday breakfast at about 3pm, followed by dinner at 5.30pm. My mother doesn't approve, my father thinks it is a big joke. I think it is neither disastrous nor funny – it's crucial.

On a school morning I usually manage to squeeze 10 minutes between my mother's and father's bathroom times. My father's reaction to anyone else being in the bathroom in 'his' bathroom time leaves much to be desired. It would be safer waving a red flag at a raging bull. I actually fear his reaction. Not that he would strike me or anything, but I think he feels both angry and hurt that he can't have the bathroom in his own home, and I wouldn't want to hurt him.

I admit I spend more than my fair share of time in the bathroom, but teenage girls need pampering time more than men. My father contradicts himself by portraying himself as an old man – too old for this and that – and then spends much time and money applying 'wet-look' styling gel to his greying locks. He unquestionably receives a fair number of jokes on this subject.

Debra McArthur, 15, lives in Wallsend, on Tyneside, where she is in form 5R1 at Burnside High School. She and her 25 classmates were set 'A Life in the Day' as an assignment in personal writing — part of their English coursework for the new General Certificate of Secondary Education. Their teacher, Joan Sjøvoll, thought the results were so good that she showed them to *The Sunday Times Magazine* (see page 69). Debra hopes to take three A-levels before going on to university

Fifteen minutes is spent on applying the Polyfilla and 15 on concreting my hair into place. No breakfast is consumed as I am far too busy for food. A rummage through the wardrobe finds my uniform and it's ready and set for action.

My father leaves five minutes earlier than usual on cold mornings so that if the car fails to start the bus is an available option – but not for me. It's simply hard lines. I'm late! Luckily (or unluckily) the car usually starts the first time.

I usually enjoy school if I'm up to date with my schoolwork. I hate the feeling of being left behind with anything. I suppose I just hate missing out, even if avoiding this entails 'hard slog'. I enjoy school mainly because of the number of friends I have there. I also hate being alone. Another good reason for coming to school is to see my boyfriend, Craig, whom I meet every lunchtime. However, I do not let this interfere with my schoolwork. I believe that if I centre my full attention on either one or the other I will lose out somewhere.

At lunchtime I either go on a binge or I starve myself – never the happy medium. I usually starve for two reasons: either to make up for the binge which took place the previous day or to save money. At Christmas I save every penny I receive in order to buy people decent gifts. When I do find I have quite a lot of money for myself it seems to affect my logic. I either give it away or buy other people things, instead of spending it on the one who earned it – me! But I do love having money to spend on myself. My father would say I waste it but I relish the thought of taking the chemist's counter by storm. It's unbelievable how quickly I can spend £20 on make-up and other such junk!

After school it's either netball practice for the school team or it's off home and tarting up time once again. I see Craig almost every evening. He says he doesn't mind what I look like but I like to feel as though I've made an effort for him. I either fit my homework in before I see him, during the time I see him, or when he leaves for the bus at 11pm – which would account for the lateness in my morning getting-up time. Either way, my homework gets done.

Aside from my uniform, my clothes are fairly general. I do not have a separate wardrobe for my 'best' clothes, although I wish I had. I sometimes wear new tops with somewhat tatty trousers, but usually I like to think I dress smartly and with some degree of taste. My Sunday best can easily be described as my Sunday worst. I wear absolutely anything I lay my hands on when I crawl out of bed on a Sunday afternoon. I babysit for my neighbour and life-long friend on a Sunday evening. (God only knows what she must think of my dress sense – or lack or it.)

I really enjoy looking after young children. They are so interesting. It was an ambition of mine to be a nanny or nursery nurse, but efforts to dissuade me eventually succeeded. 'You're too bright.' 'There's no money in it.' 'You'd get bored.' 'You'd be able to get a far better job.' I suppose I could babysit as a hobby until I have children of my own. I am looking forward very much to having children. Not actually the pregnancy and birth, but the end product. I am not keen on the idea of being a stereotypical mother/housewife. I also want a career, and a good one, but doing what? I wish I knew! My father continuously asks whether I have made up my mind yet. Now I am concentrating on gaining good exam results so that I will have a solid base from which to move in any direction – preferably upwards.

I often think about possible careers, pick them to pieces in my mind, discard the confused ideas and replace them with fantasies. I am a demon for fantasising. I still maintain that I am going to be taken and made rich and famous due to an outstanding talent yet unrevealed (as you see in the movies). My bedtime thoughts consist of these two elements. Then come the 'late-night worries' inherited from my father. I allow myself to worry about anything and everything. I worry about school, money, my future, the next day, what I look like, what people think about me and what I could do to change the way people think about me.

These are all factors which in later years will contribute to the steady increase of grey hairs. I usually wear my brain out at about 1am when I've worried myself silly and into slumberland. Peace at last!"

Next week: Richard Jobson, television and radio presenter

The Sunday Times Magazine

15

You may wish to work on all these activities, or to choose one which interests you. See Techniques on pp.18 – 19 for further help.

My life in a poem

Try to tell the entire story of your life in a poem, no longer than those on pp.10 – 11. You might use any of these lines to help you organise what you have to say:

> I was born in . . .
> I remember moments when I felt . . .
> When I was seven . . .
> It was one summer when . . .
> The first time I met . . .
> As I got older, I realised . . .
> The hardest time was . . .
> I feel now . . .
> I really hope that . . .
> In the future . . .

Comparing two poems

Here are five important elements in autobiographical writing:

- **memory triggers**
- **time clues** identifying different moments in the past.
- **story telling**
- **vivid detail** describing colours, shapes, sounds, textures, smells and perhaps tastes in the past.
- **reflections** expressing thoughts and feelings about the past.

In groups, read *Nikki-Rosa* and *Digging* aloud. Then discuss how important you feel each of the five elements are to each poem. Which poem expresses the memory of childhood more effectively, in the group's view?

Imaginative writing

Write a poem or true story in which you describe a close friend or relative from your past. Begin your writing with a memory trigger – perhaps a sound or a taste which recalls this person. Then try to bring alive the presence of the person as s/he lived and breathed – at work or doing something s/he loved. In your writing, reflect upon your relationship with this person, perhaps comparing the past with today.

Beginning an autobiography

The autobiographies of famous people are often written by *ghost writers* – professional people hired to do the writing. Try being a ghost writer, either for a famous person who interests you, or for someone you know. If you choose someone famous, find out more about their childhood and background, or imagine it. If it is someone you know, go and interview them. (See pp.**194-196** on Interviewing.)

Write the opening two pages or so of their autobiography. Using the opening to *Moonwalk* on p.12 as an example, work out how your opening might arouse your reader's interest in the *rest* of the book. This might be done by describing:

- a startling experience,
- a strong personal belief,
- a look at the future,
- a relationship which went wrong.

'A Life in the Day of...': *magazine interview*

Interview

Read *A Life in the Day of Debra McArthur* on p.15, taken from a series in *The Sunday Times Magazine* on the lifestyles of people both well-known and little known.

Imagine that *The Sunday Times* has chosen to interview a number of you for its 'A Life in the Day of...' series. A journalist from the magazine will be tape-recording the interviews.

1. In pairs, work out a set of questions the journalist will ask. Make sure that you cover a full range of topics about a person's daily lifestyle. (See p.**194-196** on Interviewing.)
2. Now decide who will be the journalist, and who will be the person being interviewed.
3. Rehearse your interview first. When both of you are happy with it, either perform it to the class, or tape-record it.

Article

Write an article based on your role play, as if for publication in *The Sunday Times*. If you were the journalist, write the article about your partner. If you were the person interviewed, write it about yourself. Entitle the article 'A Life in the Day of...' and if possible, find a photograph for it.

TECHNIQUES

Telling my own story

We all tell stories about ourselves in everyday conversation – when we gossip, joke, confide in others, confess secrets, or tell lies! There is also a long tradition of telling stories about ourselves in writing – in autobiography, diary, memoirs, poetry and song.

When you tell your own story, you should aim to use a mixture of three types of expression which characterise most autobiographical writing. These are:

1. Narrating

Narrating simply means telling a story. It is natural for people to remember what has happened to them in the form of a story or narrative. If you are recalling your past, you will probably use the past tense.

'...you always remember things like ...
how good the water felt when you got your bath from one of those big tubs that folk in chicago barbecue in ...'

If you are telling a story about your life at the moment, you will probably use the present tense.

'At roughly 7.30 am my radio alarm buzzes. As it is actually on my bed, it literally blasts me into awareness of the morning...'

2. Describing

If you describe the people and places in your story, it will help your reader, or listener, to picture your experiences more vividly.

'... My father contradicts himself by portraying himself as an old man – too old for this and that – and then spends much time and money applying 'wet-look' styling gel to his greying locks...'

3. Expressing my thoughts

If you express how you feel and think about your life, it will help your reader, or listener, to identify with your viewpoint.

'... There was a park across the street from the Motown studio, and I can remember looking at those kids playing games. I'd just stare at them in wonder – I couldn't imagine such freedom, such a carefree life – and wish more than anything that I had that kind of freedom, that I could walk away and be like them...'

Choose any one of the texts in this chapter, and see whether you can identify the three types of expression – **narrating, describing** and **reflecting** – which characterise most autobiographical writing.

2 · Narrating

The Storyteller, Marrakesh, Morocco.

STARTERS

Are we all story-tellers?

The following statements are all about stories: who tells them, who listens to them and why. In groups, discuss the statements, saying which ones you agree with, which you disagree with and why. Try to find examples to support the statements you agree with.

- *We all tell stories.*
- *Most stories are made up.*
- *Only a few people can tell stories well.*
- *Many stories are never written down.*
- *Good stories can teach you something.*

What do these terms mean?

Stories can take many different forms. In pairs, try to work out definitions of any of the following story types you do not know. Then write the 'recipe' for any *two* story types – that is, give the 'ingredients' which distinguish a folk tale from, say, a fable.

Folk tale
Nursery rhyme
Fairy tale
Fable
Myth
Legend
Parable
Ballad
Anecdote
Limerick
Soap opera
Joke

Folk tale plots

The plot outlines below are the openings of three ancient folk tales from India. In pairs, choose *one* which interests you. Then spend a few minutes jotting down some ideas to develop the story and work out how it might end. If you already know the story, plan how you might retell it as entertainingly as possible. Then in larger groups, tell (and perhaps tape-record) your own version of the story.

A Nasty Rumour
A holy man called Harasvamim, who lives by begging, is the victim of a nasty rumour. The rumour is that he has been eating all the young children in the town...

An Indian Love Story
A man in the service of the King is forced to leave his wife at home. She is distraught and begs him to return on the first day of Spring...

Mousey the Merchant
A son of a poor widow sets out to become a merchant. At the house of a rich merchant, he hears a challenge. 'Even with this mouse which you see lying dead on the floor, a clever fellow would be able to make money...'

There are many ways of narrating, or telling a story. On these pages there is a transcribed anecdote, a traditional ballad, a retelling of a well-known fairy tale, and a newspaper story. Each tells a story about the theme of this chapter: **living dangerously.**

Sukhinder's Grandmother's Story

This story was originally told in Punjabi and was recorded on to tape. Sukhinder then translated the story into English and transcribed it in this way:

When I was seven years of age my parents passed away, so my Uncle and Aunt brought me up. In our religion a festival is held every year, it is a celebration when lots of people get together, they get together and have a laugh and a joke. There's a party going around, there's food and drinks and everything and there's rides for little children; let's say there's everything for everybody so that everybody can have some fun. It's a time when everybody can get up and enjoy themselves, leave the work to a side, enjoy themselves. It is when everybody wants to go but to some circumstances some people are unable to attend, me for instance, one reason was because I was a girl and my Uncle said I wasn't old enough so he forbidded me to go to attend any festivals because one of my parents had died and he said that girls weren't allowed to wander off by themselves. When my friends came round to my house to invite me to the festival I was unable to refuse and what I said was yes, I wanted to go but without telling my Uncle and Aunt that I wanted to go on the sneak. So that night I sneaked out and attended the festival but on the way back as I was climbing over my neighbours' roof, because that was the way I went, I fell through. When I tried the door I found it was locked so I put a plank of wood on a pile of dirt and managed to clamber out. I thought I got away with it that night, until the next morning when the neighbours complained and I got a beating. Now I am sixty-five years old and when I think back I cannot imagine it that I was the same person doing all those naughty little things!

Sukhinder, The Bluecoat School, Dudley, England.

Poor but Honest

She was poor, but she was honest,
    Victim of the squire's whim:
First he loved her, then he left her,
    And she lost her honest name.

Then she ran away to London,
    For to hide her grief and shame,
There she met another squire,
    And she lost her name again.

See her riding in her carriage,
    In the Park and all so gay:
All the nibs and nobby persons
    Come to pass the time of day.

See the little old-world village
    Where her aged parents live,
Drinking the champagne she sends them;
    But they never can forgive.

In the rich man's arms she flutters,
    Like a bird with broken wing:
First he loved her, then he left her,
    And she hasn't got a ring.

See him in the splendid mansion,
    Entertaining with the best,
While the girl that he has ruined,
    Entertains a sordid guest.

See him in the House of Commons,
    Making laws to put down crime,
While the victim of his passions
    Trails her way through mud and slime.

Standing on the bridge at midnight,
    She says: 'Farewell, blighted Love.'
There's a scream, a splash – Good Heavens!
    What is she a-doing of?

Then they drag her from the river,
    Water from her clothes they wrang
For they thought that she was drownded;
    But the corpse got up and sang:

'It's the same the whole world over;
    It's the poor that gets the blame,
It's the rich that get the pleasure.
    Isn't it a blooming shame?'

Anon

The Werewolf

It is a northern country; they have cold weather, they have cold hearts.

Cold; tempest; wild beasts in the forest. It is a hard life. Their houses are built of logs, dark and smoky within. There will be a crude icon of the virgin behind a guttering candle, the leg of a pig hung up to cure, a string of drying mushrooms. A bed, a stool, a table. Harsh, brief, poor lives.

To these upland woodsmen, the Devil is as real as you or I. More so; they have not seen us nor even know that we exist, but the Devil they glimpse often in the graveyards, those bleak and touching townships of the dead where the graves are marked with portraits of the deceased in the naïf style and there are no flowers to put in front of them, no flowers grow there, so they put out small, votive offerings, little loaves, sometimes a cake that the bears come lumbering from the margins of the forest to snatch away. At midnight, especially on Walpurgisnacht, the Devil holds picnics in the graveyards and invites the witches; then they dig up fresh corpses, and eat them. Anyone will tell you that.

Wreaths of garlic on the doors keep out the vampires. A blue-eyed child born feet first on the night of St John's Eve will have second sight. When they discover a witch – some old woman whose cheeses ripen when her neighbours' do not, another old woman whose black cat, oh, sinister! *follows her about all the time*, they strip the crone, search for her marks, for the super-numerary nipple her familiar sucks. They soon find it. Then they stone her to death.

Winter and cold weather.

Go and visit grandmother, who has been sick. Take her the oatcakes I've baked for her on the hearthstone and a little pot of butter.

The good child does as her mother bids – five miles' trudge through the forest; do not leave the path because of the bears, the wild boar, the starving wolves. Here, take your father's hunting knife; you know how to use it.

The child had a scabby coat of sheepskin to keep out the cold, she knew the forest too well to fear it but she must always be on her guard. When she heard that freezing howl of a wolf, she dropped her gifts, seized her knife and turned on the beast.

It was a huge one, with red eyes and running, grizzled chops; any but a mountaineer's child would have died of fright at the sight of it. It went for her throat, as wolves do, but she made a great swipe at it with her father's knife and slashed off its right forepaw.

The wolf let out a gulp, almost a sob, when it saw what had happened to it; wolves are less brave than they seem. It went lolloping off disconsolately between the trees as well as it could on three legs, leaving a trail of blood behind it. The child wiped the blade of her knife clean on her apron, wrapped up the wolf's paw in the cloth in which her mother had packed the oatcakes and went on towards her grandmother's house. Soon it came on to snow so thickly that the path and any footsteps, track or spoor that might have been upon it were obscured.

She found her grandmother was so sick she had taken to her bed and fallen into a fretful sleep, moaning and shaking so that the child guessed she had a fever. She felt the forehead, it burned. She shook out the cloth from her basket, to use it to make the old woman a cold compress, and the wolf's paw fell to the floor.

But it was no longer a wolf's paw. It was a hand, chopped off at the wrist, a hand toughened with work and freckled with old age. There was a wedding ring on the third finger and a wart on the index finger. By the wart, she knew it for her grandmother's hand.

She pulled back the sheet but the old woman woke up, at that, and began to struggle, squawking and shrieking like a thing possessed. But the child was strong, and armed with her father's hunting knife; she managed to hold her grandmother down long enough to see the cause of her fever. There was a bloody stump where her right hand should have been, festering already.

The child crossed herself and cried out so loud the neighbours heard her and come rushing in. They knew the wart on the hand at once for a witch's nipple; they drove the old woman, in her shift as she was, out into the snow with sticks, beating her old carcass as far as the edge of the forest, and pelted her with stones until she fell down dead.

Now the child lived in her grandmother's house; she prospered.

Angela Carter

Events which are reported in the news are often told in story form. This seems to be particularly true when the event reported is a deeply emotional one. Many of the conventional techniques of story-telling or **narrating** are to be found in news stories like this one. (See Techniques on p.30 for further work on this.)

ABSEIL ESCAPE FOR 59 IN SKYRIDE HELL

A FUN park pleasure ride turned to horror when 59 people were trapped in stranded cable cars 100 feet above the ground yesterday.

Women and children screamed as high winds battered the swaying gondolas.

Some terrified families waited two hours before rescuers could inch along the cable to reach them.

Then they had to make a nightmare descent, abseiling down ropes into a wooded ravine.

"I have never been so scared in my life," said weeping passenger Bobbie Lavender, 23. "I kept thinking 'Oh God, I'm going to die'.

A boy of four was carried to safety strapped to the chest of a rescue worker.

Amazingly, no one was hurt in the drama at Alton Towers in Staffordshire, Britain's biggest amusement park.

Staff said they regularly rehearse rescues on the £6 million Skyride and everything went to plan.

The Easter holiday was only a few hours old when high winds began to threaten the two-year-old Skyride.

The gales triggered a computer alarm at 11.15am and engineers decided to close the French-built system.

But before they could evacuate all the passengers a freak gust slammed one of the gondolas against a steel support tower and a communication wire snagged on a guide wheel underneath it.

The ride stopped immediately, stranding the 59 people in the last few cars.

Firemen rescued passengers from some gondolas with turntable ladders and a hydraulic platform, but they could not reach the highest ones.

Members of the Alton Towers rescue team used Alpine techniques to make their way

by ALAN QUALTROUGH and STEVE McKENLAY

along the cables, then climbed down rope ladders into the swaying cars.

A hundred feet below them other staff cleared trees and bushes and struggled in deep mud and high winds to steady ropes the passengers were sliding down.

Rescued Miss Lavender, of Wickford, Essex, said after she landed safely: "I was sick with fright. I am terrified of heights and when I saw the rope I thought I would never be able to use it to get down.

"The Alton Towers rescue team were marvellous. Even when I thought the car was going to fall they were trying their best to make me laugh."

Her fiance Andy Hargreaves, 26, said: "I'll say I was frightened. When the wind blew the car was swinging, jolting and squeaking. I thought I was going to die."

Brian Ward, 31, of Grays, Essex, was trapped with his wife Deborah, 29, and children Ria, seven and Westley, four.

Westley was lowered to the ground strapped to the chest of a rescue worker.

Mr Ward said: "We never want to go on that ride again."

Trevor Rowbotham, 40, from Scunthorpe, abseiled down with his wife Valerie, 41, and sons Neil, 15, and Andrew, 14.

Humour

He said: "I was more frightened coming down the rope than being trapped in the car."

But Neil joked: "It was the best ride I've ever had."

Rescuer Mark Symonds, 25, who climbed into one of the cars, said: "The people were obviously relieved to see me but considering the circumstances they were in good humour.

"The operation was straightforward and went exactly to plan. We are very pleased with the outcome."

Rescue team leader Clive Stephens said they had rehearsed an emergency evacuation two weeks ago. "This was a normal shutdown procedure," he said.

Staffordshire fire chief Peter Reid was called to the scene to oversee the rescue operation.

'I have never been so scared in my life'

Divisional commander Peter Hollands said: "Rescue attempts were made more difficult by the very high winds and the difficult terrain around the ride.

"But we were aware of this possibility and have performed rescue exercises on this ride and were able to use some of the techniques today."

Alton Towers said last night the Skyride would be back in action today. "Steps have been taken to ensure that the problems cannot arise again," said a spokesman.

from *Today*

See Techniques on pp.30-33, before choosing from these activities.

Stories from home

Parents, grandparents, friends, older people in the neighbourhood, may all have fascinating stories to tell about **living dangerously**. Ask someone you know well to recall a story about their own life which s/he would be happy to tell you. You might show them the story by Sukhinder on p.22, or suggest these possibilities for topics:

- childhood pranks/upsets
- accidents
- 'dares'/risks taken/dangers encountered
- a change in life – moving job/house/country
- acts of heroism
- grand failures

If possible, tape-record the story so that you can play it back to other members of your class, or transcribe it later on. If tape-recording is not possible, see how much of the story you can remember and recall!

Transforming a ballad

Before the twentieth century, ballads were a very popular way of telling or singing a story. If a modern version of *Poor but Honest* on p.23 were to be told today, it might possibly take one of these forms:

– a soap opera
– a news story
– a 'hit single' with video
– a mini-drama series or even a TV advert for a charity such as Shelter

In groups, read the ballad aloud two or three times. Then work out a role play using the whole, or part, of the original story in the ballad, but presenting it in one of the modern forms above. For example, your group might choose to mime the story in the poem as if it is a video for a 'hit single'. Or the group might act out a news item on television which reports on the case of a tragic suicide.

Writing a ballad

Try 'composing' a ballad of your own, choosing one of these subjects or one similar:

a modern day version :	the rise and fall of a young man or woman from a poor background.
a traditional tale :	a similar story to *Poor but Honest* about the tragedy of a young man.
a happy version :	a similar story to *Poor but Honest* but with a heroine who makes her fortune/gets her revenge/helps other poor people.

When you write your own ballad, aim to use a similar rhythm and rhyming scheme to the original. Note that the rhythm has a pattern of alternately stressed, then unstressed syllables. Also, the last words of the second and fourth verses should rhyme, like this:

> Sée her ríding ín her cárriage
> Ín the Párk and áll so gáy,
> Áll the níbs and nóbby pérsons
> Cóme to páss the tíme of dáy

Folk and fairy tales

Angela Carter's story, *The Werewolf*, on pp.24-25 is a version of *Little Red Riding Hood*. It is clearly not written for young children, but for older readers. Try to find an original version of the tale and in groups discuss what differences there are in the use of plot, setting, character, viewpoint and message.

Choose a folk or fairy tale which you can recall from your childhood, and if possible, find an original version of this tale from home, or from a library. Then create your own version of this tale, not for children but for older readers. Keep the plot itself as close as possible to the original tale, but aim to vary one or more of these narrative elements:

Setting
a modern city?
the future?
a very hot/cold country?
a definite past: e.g. Second World War, Victorian Times?

Character
'world-wise' children?
adults?
aliens from outer space?

Viewpoint
a feminist narrator who believes strong women should triumph over weak men?
an 'animal rights' supporter who wants animals to triumph over humans?

Message
a political point?
a topical message relating to an item in the news?

When you have written your tale, read it either to people in your own class, or to members of another class. See whether anyone can guess which original tale you are 'rewriting'. Can they spot the various ways in which you have changed the original tale?

Narrating

For the advice which follows, refer both to *The Werewolf* (p.24) and *Abseil Escape* (p.27).

When you are telling a story *aloud*, whether true or fictional, you can use your voice, face and hands to express and emphasise parts of your story.

When you are telling a story *in writing*, you have to rely on the power of language to bring alive the action, characters, setting and ideas. The style you use will depend very much on the *genre* or type of story you tell: e.g. anecdote, ballad, folk tale and newspaper story. There are four different genres, each with their own conventions determining how they should be written. Whatever the genre, your story will contain a number of common narrative elements, as follows:

1. Setting

Decide how you will locate your story in time and space. Look, for example, at the opening sentences of the short story and the news 'story':

> *It is a northern country; they have cold weather, they have cold hearts.*
>
> (from *The Werewolf*)
>
> *A fun park pleasure ride turned to horror when 59 people were trapped in cable cars 100 feet above the ground yesterday.*
>
> (from *Abseil Escape*)

- How much information does each opening sentence give you about where and when each story is set?
- Why do you think that the short story gives more attention to describing the setting than the news story?

2. Viewpoint

Now decide who is narrating your story.

> *A fun park pleasure ride turned to horror when 59 people were trapped in stranded cable cars 100 feet above the ground yesterday.*
>
> *I'll say I was frightened. When the wind blew, the car was swinging, jolting and squeaking. I thought I was going to die.*
>
> (from *Abseil Escape*)

- Who is the first narrator?
- Who is the second narrator?
- How were you able to tell in each case?
- Why do you think there are differences in the way each narrator tells the same story?

More often stories are told as if the narrator is standing outside the action and is not personally involved. So it is narrated in the third person (he/she). Sometimes stories are written in the first person, ('I') where the narrator plays a part in the story.

- Write a paragraph describing the rescue from the cable car as if you were one of the trapped people named in the news story.
- How is the impact of the story altered by telling it in first person?

3. Message

Think about whether your story will have a moral or message – an obvious reason why the story is being told. Traditional folk and fairy tales often have a clear moral, but many modern texts do not. They prefer to express a variety of ideas, themes and questions.

- *The Werewolf* is written by a contemporary writer. Is it possible to summarise the message of her version of the fairy tale?
- Does *Abseil Escape* have a message?

4. Plot : sequence

Decide in which order or *sequence* you will place the number of events in your story. It is common to tell a story in the order in which it happens – that is, *chronologically*.

The events of the *Abseil Escape* news story happened in this order:

| 1 High winds threaten Skyride | 2 Freak gusts slam a gondola against a support tower | 3 Rescue team climbs along cables and into swaying cars | 4 Passengers abseil down ropes to safety |

Now reread *Abseil Escape*.
- Is the incident told in the order in which it really happened? Try plotting the order of events on a diagram like the one above, to work out the time sequence used.
- Why might the news reporters have chosen to tell the events in the order they do?
- Write the first paragraph of the Safety Officer's report on the episode. In which order would the events be recorded?

Plot : tense

When you narrate, you usually tell what has happened in the past. Occasionally writers tell what is happening in the present. Two reasons for doing this are: 1), to heighten the dramatic effect and 2), to describe aspects of life which go on before, during and after the events of the story:

> PAST   *Women and children **screamed** as high winds **battered** the swaying gondolas. The wolf **let out** a gulp, almost a sob, when it **saw** what **happened** to it.*
>
> PRESENT 1   *Women and children **scream** as high winds **batter** the swaying gondolas.*
>   2   *It **is** a hard life. Their houses **are** built of logs, dark and smoky within.*

- Tell a partner, in the present tense, about something which happened to you earlier today. How easy is this to maintain?
- How does the present tense alter the effect of what you are saying?

Plot : describing action

Think about how you can describe the *action* in your story dramatically. This may help your reader to identify with what happens. Look at some of the describing words used to dramatise the action in *Abseil Escape*:

> *trapped*
> *screamed*
> *battered*
> *slammed*
> *snagged*
>
> **stranded** *cable cars*
> **high** *winds*
> **terrified** *families*
> **nightmare** *descent*
> **wooded** *ravine*

- Write the first paragraph of a newspaper article headlined, 'SHIP SINKS!' – where everybody is saved. Imagine your editor has asked you to write 'a good story' by describing the event dramatically.

5. Audience

When you tell a story, either in writing or aloud, think about who will be reading or listening to it.

- Imagine that you were one of the many holiday-makers trapped in the cable car and your ordeal is now over. Explain what happened to: a friend, a younger child, a journalist.
- How have you adapted your account in each case?

3 · Describing people

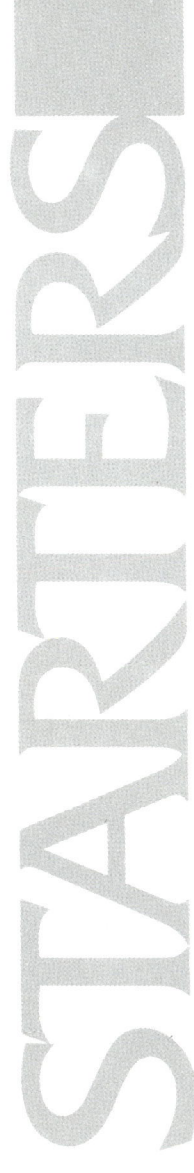

Guess who?

How well are you able to describe other people? On your own, think of two or three famous people – say, a pop musician, actor, television or sports personality, politician or member of the royal family. Then make some notes for a short description of each person, using this checklist:

Now, in groups, take turns to give a description of a famous person. You might give a clue to their profession if appropriate. The rest of the group should try to guess who you are describing.

> **facial features**
> skin
> eyes
> nose
> mouth
> hair style
>
> **physique**
> size
> height
> shape of body
>
> **clothes**
> how clothes are worn
> taste in clothes
>
> **mannerisms**
> characteristic fidgets
> gestures
> movements

Describing me

In pairs, describe how you look and feel when you are at your best. On which occasions are you at your best?

Now describe how you look and feel at your worst. When do you tend to be at your worst?

How might other people describe you? Write a short description of yourself as if you are *one* of these people: a parent, sister/brother, teacher, a grandparent, a close friend. In pairs discuss how similar or different it is from your own description and why this might be.

Describing other people

Look at these poems which describe people in the way the Chinese call 'trimmed to the bone':

> Now write your own four-line poem describing either somebody you know well, or a local 'character' you may know less well.

Swagman
Wandering, roaming,
Just whiskers, skin and bone,
Out on the dusty trail,
All alone.

    County lady
    Trotting, snorting,
    double chinned and stout,
    takes a sip of whisky,
    soothes her gout.

        Jim
        Loafing, swearing,
        Lithe, lean and hard,
        Lounges behind the bike shed,
        Late again.

The Welcome Table
for sister Clara Ward

I'm going to sit at the Welcome table
Shout my troubles over
Walk and talk with Jesus
Tell God how you treat me
One of these days!

— Spiritual

The old woman stood with eyes uplifted in her Sunday-go-to-meeting clothes: high shoes polished about the tops and toes, a long rusty dress adorned with an old corsage, long withered, and the remnants of an elegant silk scarf as headrag stained with grease from the many oily pigtails underneath. Perhaps she had known suffering. There was a dazed and sleepy look in her aged blue-brown eyes. But for those who searched hastily for "reasons" in that old tight face, shut now like an ancient door, there was nothing to be read. And so they gazed nakedly upon their own fear transferred; a fear of the black and the old, a terror of the unknown as well as of the deeply known. Some of those who saw her there on the church steps spoke words about her that were hardly fit to be heard, others held their pious peace; and some felt vague stirrings of pity, small and persistent and hazy, as if she were an old collie turned out to die.

She was angular and lean and the color of poor gray Georgia earth, beaten by king cotton and the extreme weather. Her elbows were wrinkled and thick, the skin ashen but durable, like the bark of old pines. On her face centuries were folded into the circles around one eye, while around the other, etched and mapped as if for print, ages more threatened again to live. Some of them there at the church saw the age, the dotage, the missing buttons down the front of her mildewed black dress. Others saw cooks, chauffeurs, maids, mistresses, children denied or smothered in the deferential way she held her cheek to the side, toward the ground. Many of them saw jungle orgies in an evil place, while others were reminded of riotous anarchists looting and raping in the streets. Those who knew the hesitant creeping up on them of the law, saw the beginning of the end of the sanctuary of Christian worship, saw the desecration of Holy Church, and saw an invasion of privacy, which they struggled to believe they still kept.

Still she had come down the road toward the big white church alone. Just herself, an old forgetful woman, nearly blind with age. Just her and her eyes raised dully to the glittering cross that crowned the sheer silver steeple. She had walked along the road in a stagger from her house a half mile away. Perspiration, cold and clammy, stood on her brow and along the creases by her thin wasted nose. She stopped to calm herself on the wide front steps, not looking about her as they might have expected her to do, but simply standing quite still, except for a slight quivering of her throat and tremors that shook her cotton-stockinged legs.

The reverend of the church stopped her pleasantly as she stepped into the vestibule. Did he say, as they thought he did, kindly, "Auntie, you know this is not your church"? As if one could choose the wrong one. But no one remembers, for they never spoke of it afterward, and she brushed past him anyway, as if she had been brushing past him all her life, except this time she was in a hurry. Inside the church she sat on the very first bench from the back, gazing with concentration at the stained-glass window over her head. It was cold, even inside the church, and she was shivering. Everybody could see. They stared at her as they came in and sat down near the front. It was cold, very cold to them, too; outside the church it was below freezing and not much above inside. But the sight of her, sitting there somehow passionately ignoring them, brought them up short, burning.

The young usher, never having turned anyone out of his church before, but not even considering this job as *that* (after all she had no right to be there, certainly), went up to her and whispered that she should leave. Did he call her "Grandma," as later he seemed to recall he had? But for those who actually hear such traditional pleasantries and to whom they actually mean something, "Grandma" was not one, for she did not pay him any attention, just muttered, "Go 'way," in a weak sharp *bothered* voice, waving his frozen blond hair and eyes from near her face.

It was the ladies who finally did what to them had to be done. Daring their burly indecisive husbands to throw the old colored woman out they made their point. God, mother, country, earth, church. It involved all that, and well they knew it. Leather bagged and shoed, with good calfskin gloves to keep out the cold, they looked with contempt at the bloodless gray arthritic hands of the old woman, clenched loosely, restlessly in her lap. Could their husbands expect them to sit up in church with *that*? No, no, the husbands were quick to answer and even quicker to do their duty.

Under the old woman's arms they placed their hard fists (which afterward smelled of decay and musk – the fermenting scent of onionskins and rotting greens). Under the old woman's arms they raised their fists, flexed their muscular shoulders, and out she flew through the door, back under the cold blue sky. This done, the wives folded their healthy arms across their trim middles and felt at once justified and scornful. But none of them said so, for none of them ever spoke of the incident again. Inside the church it was warmer. They sang, they prayed. The protection and promise of God's impartial love grew more not less desirable as the sermon gathered fury and lashed itself out above their penitent heads.

The old woman stood at the top of the steps looking about in bewilderment. She had been singing in her head. They had interrupted her. Promptly she began to sing again, though this time a sad song. Suddenly, however, she looked down the long gray highway and saw something interesting and delightful coming. She started to grin, toothlessly, with short giggles of joy, jumping about and slapping her hands on her knees. And soon it became apparent why she was so happy. For coming down the highway at a firm though leisurely pace was Jesus. He was wearing an immaculate white, long dress trimmed in gold around the neck and hem, and a red, a bright red, cape. Over his left arm he carried a brilliant blue blanket. He was wearing sandals and a beard and he had long brown hair parted on the right side. His eyes, brown, had wrinkles around them as if he smiled or looked at the sun a lot. She would have known him, recognized him, anywhere. There was a sad but joyful look to his face, like a candle was glowing behind it, and he walked with sure even steps in her direction, as if he were walking on the sea. Except that he was not carrying in his arms a baby sheep, he looked exactly like the picture of him that she had hanging over her bed at home. She had taken it out of a white lady's Bible while she was working for her. She had looked at that picture for more years than she could remember, but never once had she really expected to see him. She squinted her eyes to be sure he wasn't carrying a little sheep in one arm, but he was not. Ecstatically she began to wave her arms for fear he would miss seeing her, for he walked looking straight ahead on the shoulder of the highway, and from time to time looking upward at the sky.

All he said when he got up close to her was "Follow me," and she bounded down to his side with all the bob and speed of one so old. For every one of his long determined steps she made two quick ones. They walked along in deep silence for a long time. Finally she started telling him about how many years she had cooked for them, cleaned for them, nursed them. He looked at her kindly but in silence. She told him indignantly about how they had grabbed her when she was singing in her head and not looking, and how they had tossed her out of his church. A old heifer like me, she said, straightening up next to Jesus, breathing hard. But he smiled down at her and she felt better instantly and time just seemed to fly by. When they passed her house, forlorn and sagging, weatherbeaten and patched, by the side of the road, she did not even notice it, she was so happy to be out walking along the highway with Jesus.

She broke the silence once more to tell Jesus how glad she was that he had come, how she had often looked at his picture hanging on her wall (she hoped he didn't know she had stolen it) over her bed, and how she had never expected to see him down here in person. Jesus gave her one of his beautiful smiles and they walked on. She did not know where they were going; someplace wonderful, she suspected. The ground was like clouds under their feet, and she felt she could walk forever without becoming the least bit tired. She even began to sing out loud some of the old spirituals she loved, but she didn't want to annoy Jesus, who looked so thoughtful, so she quieted down. They walked on, looking straight over the treetops into the sky, and the smiles that played over her dry wind-cracked face were like first clean ripples across a stagnant pond. On they walked without stopping.

The people in church never knew what happened to the old woman; they never mentioned her to one another or to anybody else. Most of them heard sometime later that an old colored woman fell dead along the highway. Silly as it seemed, it appeared she had walked herself to death. Many of the black families along the road said they had seen the old lady high-stepping down the highway; sometimes jabbering in a low insistent voice, sometimes singing, sometimes merely gesturing excitedly with her hands. Other times silent and smiling, looking at the sky. She had been alone, they said. Some of them wondered aloud where the old woman had been going so stoutly that it had worn her heart out. They guessed maybe she had relatives across the river, some miles away, but none of them really knew.

Alice Walker, a short story from *In Love and Trouble.*

ACTIVITIES

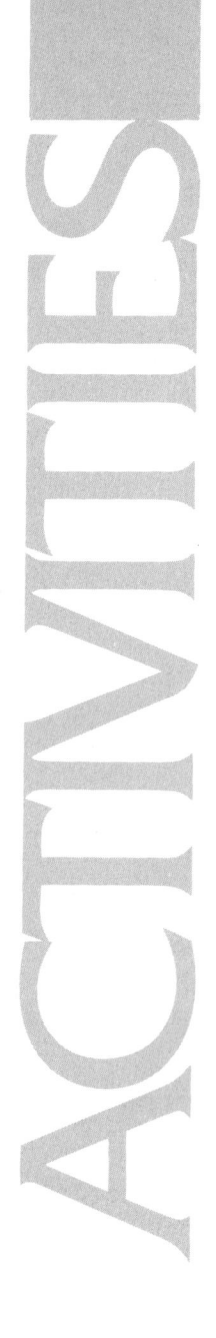

Describing myself

Write a description of yourself using the pictures on p.34, as a guide. The idea is to describe as many aspects of yourself as possible. For example, start each new paragraph by describing how different moods affect and change you (*left*). Or compare the way you appear to others with the way you really are (*right*):

> When I am relaxed ...   I often appear to be ...
> When I am angry ...
> When I am tired ...   ... But really I am ...
> When I am impatient ...
> When I am nervous ...

Describing a person

Describe an episode in the life of an old person, either real or imaginary, who has been a victim of hardship but who has managed to retain some dignity. For example you might choose:

> – a country or a city tramp
> – a street corner trader: 'the newspaper seller', 'the busker', 'the flower woman'.

In telling your story, describe the appearance and lifestyle of this person as fully as possible, as well as the attitude of people towards him/her.

Role play

If you have access to a drama room or similar space to move around, try acting out two versions of *The Welcome Table*.

In large groups, share out the roles of the old woman, the reverend, the usher, and the members of the congregation. Then reread the first part of the story, in order to work out how you will dramatise each version. In both versions think carefully about how you will show the impact the old woman has upon the church congregation.

Version 1
Follow the text closely to work out a play version of the first half of the story, in which the old woman enters the church, then is thrown out by 'the husbands'.

Version 2
Work out an alternative version of the same sequence of events. This time show the reverend and the congregation reacting to the old woman in quite a different way.

Understanding

The old woman in *The Welcome Table* is so vividly described that it is possible to imagine her as a real person. In fact, her character is only a fictional device – important for the part it plays in a story. So the *way* the old woman's character is described will provide clues to the events which are to follow.

Read each of these quotations from the story carefully:

> *'... The old woman stood with eyes uplifted in her Sunday-go-to-meeting clothes; high shoes polished about the tops and toes, a long rusty dress adorned with an old corsage, long withered, and the remnants of an elegant silk scarf as headrag stained with grease from the many oily pigtails underneath...'*
>
> *'... She was angular and lean and the color of poor gray Georgia earth, beaten by king cotton and the extreme weather. Her elbows were wrinkled and thick, the skin ashen and durable, like the bark of old pines. On her face centuries were folded into the circles around one eye, while around the other, etched and mapped as if for print, ages more threatened again to live...'*
>
> *'... Perspiration, cold and clammy, stood on her brow and along the creases by her thin wasted nose. She stopped to calm herself on the wide front steps, not looking about her as they might have expected her to do, but simply standing quite still, except for a slight quivering of her throat and tremors that shook her cotton-stockinged legs...'*

In groups, look at each of the quotations in turn, and discuss how the language gives you clues about:

a) the old woman's state of mind, and, perhaps, her closeness to death.
b) the effect she has on other characters in the story, which causes them to behave as they do.

Alternative point of view

Write about what happens in *The Welcome Table* from the point of view of another character in the story – for example, a member of the congregation, the young usher or the reverend of the church.

As this person, give your impressions of the old woman's appearance and behaviour, and express why you feel and behave towards her as you do. What is your reaction later on to the news of her death on the highway?

TECHNIQUES

Describing people

When you describe a person, it is as if you are creating a picture in words.

'... Perhaps she had known suffering. There was a dazed and sleepy look in her aged, blue-brown eyes...'

Sometimes a description can be far more powerful than a picture because we seem to sense that the person being described is real. You can describe people vividly by using:

1. The Five Senses

The Welcome Table stimulates several of our five senses to the point that we can almost see, touch, hear and smell the old woman. Her appearance is partly suggested by *shape* and *colour*:

'... She was angular and lean and the color of poor gray Georgia earth...'

But a stronger impression of why she repels the members of the congregation is indicated by *smell*:

'... Under the old woman's arms they placed their hard fists (which afterward smelled of decay and musk – the fermenting scent of onionskins and rotting greens...'

- Look at the description of Jesus on p.38. To which of our senses does Alice Walker appeal and why might she wish to do this here?
- Find examples from the story of words or phrases which describe the *texture* of the old woman's skin – the way it felt to the touch.
- What impressions do we have of the old woman's voice and the sounds she makes? How important do you think these are to the story?

2. Vivid vocabulary

Choose describing words which give a precise and vivid sense of a person as an *individual*.

In *The Welcome Table*, notice how the old woman's body is not described as 'thin' but as 'angular and lean'. Her clothes are not simply described as 'old', but 'rusty', 'long withered', 'stained with grease' and later, 'mildewed'.

- What do these adjectives tell us about the old woman other than that her clothes are old?

A thesaurus will help you to widen your vocabulary and to use less obvious and more precise words. But do not try to be too clever about it – short, simple words are usually more effective than complex ones!

3. Comparisons

Sometimes you can describe the qualities of a person more imaginatively if you use comparisons. This technique is known as *imagery* or *figurative writing*. There are two common types of comparison:

Simile is where you compare one thing with another thing, using the link words 'like' or 'as'.

> '...Her elbows were wrinkled and thick... **like** the bark of old pines...'

- Which two things are being compared in this simile and why?
- Find *one* more simile used to describe the old woman and explain it.
- Find *two* similes used to describe Jesus and explain them.

Metaphor is where one thing is presented as being another thing. It is not *like* something else, it *is* that other thing. There are no link words to join the two halves of the comparison. If the example of a simile (above), were to become a metaphor, it would read:

> Her elbow **was** the bark of old pines.

- Can you find any examples of metaphor used to describe the old woman?

4 · Describing places

Midsummer, Tobago

Broad sun-stoned beaches.

White heat.
A green river.

A bridge,
scorched yellow palms

from the summer-sleeping house
drowsing through August.

Days I have held,
days I have lost,

days that outgrow, like daughters,
my harbouring arms.

Derek Walcott

STARTERS

Describing a place through mime

If you have some space to move around, describe a place through mime. In groups, take turns to choose at random, and then mime what it would be like to go into one of these houses/homes:

- derelict
- luxurious
- 'brand new'
- untidy
- haunted
- empty
- old-fashioned
- high-rise
- stately
- tropical/arctic

The group should try to guess which type of home each of you is miming.

Selling your school

Imagine that your school is up for sale and that you are working for the estate agent who is selling it. Suppose that *one* of the following is interested in buying it.

- a hotel
- a leisure centre
- a private hospital
- a computer firm
- a television company
- the prison service

You have to think of all the selling points about the school – the features which might recommend it to your client. In pairs, select one client from the list above, then write a short and flattering description of your school, pointing out its potential for conversion.

Describing the place where you live

Read these two poems by students:

> **Goole, Humberside, England**
> The fish stink
> Ships come to and fro
> Loaded with Carlsberg beer,
> Docks are scattered around,
> Rainbows on the water as oil floats by.
>
> **Karachi, Pakistan**
> Motor-powered rickshaws
> Camels in the street
> Parched scrubland all around;
> Mosquitoes,
> Houses squashed in
> People jammed.

Write a short poem describing your own village, town, city or country. Do not mention directly the name of the place you are writing about except in the title. Try to give the outstanding features of this place so that anyone familiar with it might be able to guess the location.

S. STATE & CO.

Tenure:
- * LEASEHOLD
- * ONE BEDROOM
- * COMPACT KITCHEN
- * MODERN BATHROOM
- * VERSATILE LOUNGE
- * ECONOMY 7 HEATING
- * PERMIT HOLDER PARKING
- * TOWN CENTRE LOCATION

Address: Flat 4, 88 Lowland Avenue, Upshott, Notts.

To be sold: Set in the popular Church Lane area of Upshott, No. 88 gives easy access to the town's comprehensive shopping facilities and is in walking distance of the main line station.

Accommodation comprises:

Security entrance to communal hall, private door to hardwood front door with peep-hole.
ENTRANCE : Wall mounted security phone, artex ceiling, doors to all rooms.
KITCHEN : Comprising of single drainer stainless steel sink unit with tiled splash back, cupboards under, electric cooker power points, strip lighting, artex ceiling.
BATHROOM : Comprising of panel enclosed bath with courtesy handrails, pedestal hand basin with tiled splash back, towel rail, wall mounted electric lighting, extractor fan, artex ceiling.
LOUNGE/BEDROOM : (15' x 8') Double aspect, economy 7 storage heater, airing cupboard housing lagged copper cylinder tank with shelving around, artex ceiling and ample power points.
VIEWING: Strictly by appointment throug the Vendors Sole Agents S. State & Co.

S. STATE & CO.

Address: 'Penhurst', 16 Lowland Drive, Upshott, Notts.

Tenure: A WEALTH OF CHARACTER * 3 SPACIOUS BEDROOMS * SUPERB FAMILY
           BATHROOM/ENSUITE SHOWER * 2 MAGNIFICENT BEAMED RECEPTION ROOMS *
           EXCELLENT FULLY-FITTED FRENCH STYLE KITCHEN * GAS CENTRAL HEATING
           AND DOUBLE-GLAZED DOORS * 100 FT SOUTH FACING REAR GARDEN *
           A STONE'S THROW FROM LOCAL SHOPS *

To be sold: Penhurst is a most attractive 1969 character built cottage style
home in much-sought after village location. The property, which has been
fully and tastefully refurbished with total replumbing done four years ago and
new boiler, features a magnificent French Style antique pine kitchen, beamed
drawing room with an open fireplace, three large bedrooms, ensuite and a
whisper pink family bathroom with a corner bath all with oak panelled doors
and floors. An early inspection is recommended.

Accommodation comprises:

LARGE ENTRANCE HALL : With radiator, central heating thermostat, cloakroom
with low-level WC, radiator.
DRAWING ROOM : (19' x 13'5) Original open brick fireplace with ornamental
brick and tiled hearth, adjoining gas point, flanking oak shelving, oak
bressumer, TV point, two radiators, patio doors opening to sun terrace
and garden, study area with views down the garden, artexed ceiling.
DINING ROOM : (13' x 12') Double-glazed leaded light windows, radiator,
original brick feature fireplace.
DOUBLE-ASPECT KITCHEN ; (17' x 8') Quality range of antique pine, French
style units comprising of colour-keyed ceramic sink with Victorian brass
mixer taps, handles, marble effect worktops, full range of fitted cupboards
below, electronic microwave, four ring gas hob with extractor fan above,
built in dishwasher, carpet tiled floor, TV point, beamed ciling, door to back garden.

From the main entrance hall, stairway to:

FIRST FLOOR LANDING : Doors to:
MASTER BEDROOM : (13 x 14') BT point, double-glazed windows, radiator, door
to ensuite full tiled avocado shower cubicle with mixer fittings.
BEDROOM 2 : (13' x 9'9) Frontal aspect window, radiator, triple built-in
wardrobe, concealed lighting, wash hand basin.
BEDROOM 3 : (9'2 x 8'2) Rear aspect window, radiator, walk-in wardrobe, TV point.
FAMILY BEDROOM : Luxuriously fitted with corner oval bath with gold-plated
mixer taps, mirrored walls, vanitory hand basin, marble-effect taps, low-level
WC, two wall light point, radiator, shaver sockets.
TO THE FRONT OF THE PROPERTY : Pleasant sized frontage being very well-maintained
with flower beds and mature shrubs, driveway to separate garage.
TO THE REAR OF THE PROPERTY : Grounds are south facing extending to 100 ft
and mainly laid to lawn, with barbecue area and security flood-lights. The
gardens afford a substantial measure of privacy.
VIEWING : Strictly by appointment through the Vendors Sole Agents S. State & Co.

South Side

Newspapers and crisp packets
Drunk men with dirty jackets
Old cars with tyres stripped
Rubbish heaps where junk's been tipped
On the South side of the Thames.

Dirty faces, wearing rags
Used matches and ends of fags
Smoke and dirt from old cars
Smashed bottles and cracked jars
On the South side of the Thames.

Old tunnels full of dirt
Old people watching, feelings hurt
Grey walls full of graffiti
Big kids strong and meaty
On the South side of the Thames.

Broken street-lamp lights the night
Two youths quarrel and have a fight
Rag and bone men on horses and carts
Smoke in the pubs and the sound of darts
On the South side of the Thames.

Brown leaves, shrivelled flowers in a window box
Old ladies with nylon coats, wishing they were fox
Terraced houses pushing out smoke
Kids drinking water, wishing it was Coke
On the South side of the Thames.

James Smith

> "This poem was written as a piece of homework. I was asked by my English teacher to write a poem entitled 'On the South Side of the Thames'. I later changed this title to 'South Side'. This meant I had a chance to put down on paper all the little things I have noticed walking through the streets of south London. I must say though, that in this poem I have only put down the bad things about south London. There are a lot of good things I can think about it. I might even go on to write a poem including the good things about south London. I will have to see whether I get round to it."

The Deserted House

The house was left; the house was deserted. It was left like a shell on a sandhill to fill with dry salt grains now that life had left it. The long night seemed to have set in; the trifling airs, nibbling, the clammy breaths, fumbling, seemed to have triumphed. The saucepan had rusted and the mat decayed. Toads had nosed their way in. Idly, aimlessly, the swaying shawl swung to and fro. A thistle thrust itself between the tiles in the larder. The swallows nested in the drawing-room; the floor was strewn with straw; the plaster fell in shovelfuls; rafters were laid bare; rats carried off this and that to gnaw behind the wainscots. Tortoise-shell butterflies burst from the chrysalis and pattered their life out on the window-pane. Poppies sowed themselves among the dahlias; the lawn waved with long grass; giant artichokes towered among roses; a fringed carnation flowered among the cabbages; while the gentle tapping of a weed at the window had become, on winters' nights, a drumming from sturdy trees and thorned briars which made the whole room green in summer.

What power could now prevent the fertility, the insensibility of nature? Mrs McNab's dream of a lady, of a child, of a plate of milk soup? It had wavered over the walls like a spot of sunlight and vanished. She had locked the door; she had gone. It was beyond the strength of one woman, she said. They never sent. They never wrote. There were things up there rotting in the drawers – it was a shame to leave them so, she said. The place was gone to rack and ruin. Only the Lighthouse beam entered the rooms for a moment, sent its sudden stare over bed and wall in the darkness of winter, looked with equanimity at the thistle and the swallow, the rat and the straw. Nothing now withstood them; nothing said no to them. Let the wind blow; let the poppy seed itself and the carnation mate with the cabbage. Let the swallow build in the drawing-room, and the thistle thrust aside the tiles, and the butterfly sun itself on the faded chintz of the armchairs. Let the broken glass and the china lie out on the lawn and be tangled over with grass and wild berries.

For now had come that moment, that hesitation when dawn trembles and night pauses, when if a feather alight in the scale it will be weighed down. One feather, and the house, sinking, falling, would have turned and pitched downwards to the depths of darkness. In the ruined room, picnickers would have lit their kettles; lovers sought shelter there, lying on the bare boards; and the shepherd stored his dinner on the bricks; and the tramp slept with his coat round him to ward off the cold. Then the roof would have fallen; briars and hemlocks would have blotted out path, step, and window; would have grown, unequally but lustily over the mound, until some trespasser, losing his way, could have told only by a red-hot poker among the nettles, or a scrap of china in the hemlock, that here once someone had lived; there had been a house.

Virginia Woolf, from *To The Lighthouse*

ACTIVITIES

Case study : The estate agency

Please read carefully the two house descriptions on pp.46-47 before starting this case study. Consider inviting a local estate agent to talk to your class about the process of buying and selling a house. Some of you might visit a local estate agent's office to ask for a selection of house particulars and for a folder to put them into. Most estate agents should be willing to help if you explain the work you are doing.

Imagine that a group of you are setting up an estate agent's office near where you live. It is to be a small, independent company which aims to meet fairly specialised needs.

In a group of at least four, decide how to share out the work to be done for Stage 1 below.

Stage 1 : preparation

1. Decide on a name and logo for your estate agency. Work out a short slogan which advertises the main policy of your company. Then design and make a folder which advertises your company name, logo and slogan. Perhaps draw a neat map on the back cover of the folder which shows your clients where your office is located.
2. Design a postcard-sized form upon which you can enter all the details of a client. (Alternatively design a matrix for a computer database.) The form should provide space for:

> name
> address
> telephone number(s)
> type of accommodation
> price range

Consider 'type of accommodation' very carefully. Look at the different types of home (in **3** below) which clients are looking for, then decide how your form might categorise these. When you have designed your form, make several copies.

3. Design, draft, then write or type house descriptions for at least four different types of client. Some examples might be:

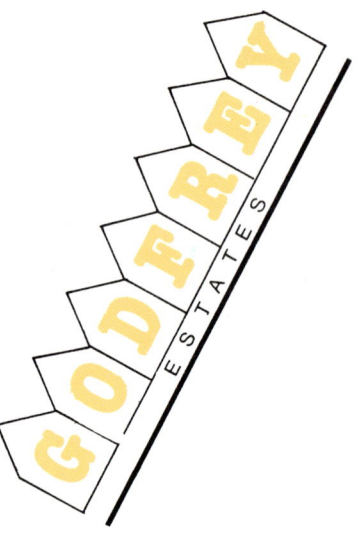

- two friends looking for a small flat to share,
- a newly married couple looking for a cheap place to 'do up',
- a sports personality wanting a small second home, with room for a gym – for example, a city penthouse, or a country cottage,
- a struggling musician or artist wanting a bedsit 'studio'.

Stage 2 : role play

Now work with another group. Take turns to play the estate agents and the clients. As **clients,** work out who each of you will play, then 'visit' the estate agent to discuss whether it has a property which might interest you. As **estate agents,** each of you will interview a client and take down details of his/her needs on the specially prepared form. Then aim to interest the client in a suitable property. The success of the exercise will depend on whether your client agrees to look at the property!

* * * * *

Read the poems *Midsummer, Tobago* and *South Side,* and the passage *The Deserted House,* all in this chapter. (Also see Techniques on p.52). Then choose one of the following activities for individual work.

The deserted house / the derelict building

Describe a deserted or derelict place you know, or can imagine, either in the city, *or* in the country.

You might wish to describe objects left behind in the building which recall the lives of the people who once lived there – an old hairbrush or a broken doll...

Two ladies clean

Just after the passage *The Deserted House* on page 49, Virginia Woolf tells of the arrival of two cleaning ladies. Their job is to make the house ready for the return of the Ramsay family.

> '...Mrs McNab groaned; Mrs Bast creaked. They were old; they were stiff; their legs ached. They came with their brooms and their pails at last; they got to work...'

Continue and finish this chapter, describing how the two cleaning ladies make the house habitable. Through their conversation, reveal what the ladies know about the Ramsay family from the objects in their house.

Poem about a place

Write a poem describing the area in which you live. Try to spend some time looking at where you live with fresh eyes, noting down details which make most impression on you. Using the poem *South Side* as a guide, decide whether you wish to concentrate on the good things about where you live, or the bad. Alternatively write about how the good and the bad elements coexist. Like James Smith, you may wish to put some comments at the foot of your poem, about the approach you have used.

Describing places

1. Selecting a focus

In any scene you wish to describe, there is so much you might notice. Some people may take in a panoramic view, others may select details. No two people will view the same place in quite the same way.

Find a focus by:

Selecting a view

If you choose a subject to describe like *The Deserted House*, the view you take is largely determined by the title. With a broader title like *Poem about a place*, you will need to select a view: panoramic, vista, 'walkabout', one specific street or square, and so on.

Selecting a theme

Choose a particular theme or idea when you describe a place: for example, the contrast between a noisy street and an empty house; the way nature gradually takes over a deserted house, and so on.

2. Concrete detail

Create the atmosphere of the place you are describing by using concrete detail. If it is a place you know, try walking about it, or sitting down to observe it. Then take notes about anything you particularly notice. In *South Side* on p.48, the writer may have prepared his poem by listing things he observed, such as:

> newspapers
> crisp packets
> drunk men
> dirty jackets
> old cars with
>   tyres stripped

3. Imagery

When you describe a place, try to use colourful comparisons. This will help your reader to visualise the place you are writing about. In *The Deserted House*, Virginia Woolf stimulates our imagination with **similes** and **metaphors**:

'...The house...was left **like a shell on a sandhill to fill with dry grains now that life had left it**...'

'...**The lawn waved** with long grass; giant artichokes **towered** among roses...'

She also uses **personification** – attributing personal qualities to the non-human world – to give the impression that nature has an almost human life force:

'...the trifling airs **nibbling**, the **clammy breaths fumbling**, seemed to have triumphed...'

4. Sound effects

You will create a vivid impression of a place by appealing to your reader's sense of sound. In *The Deserted House*, Woolf uses **onomatopoeia** – words which echo the real sounds:

'...Tortoise-shell butterflies **burst** from the chrysalis and **pattered** their life out on the window pane...'

Read this sentence aloud and listen to the poetic rhythm used here to create the sound and the movement of the butterflies. (See p.**89**.)

> Look at the sentence beginning ...*Poppies sowed themselves among the dahlias; the lawn waved*...' and consider how the following techniques help to convey the sense of nature taking over a house: the long sentence with its chain of clauses; concrete detail; imagery; sound effects.

5 · Living English

Compliment or insult?

People who come from a particular area and who speak in a distinctive way may be given several different names. Here are some well-known examples:

> Scouse
> Aussie
> Brummie
> Pom
> Paddy
> Jock
> Taffy
> Yorky
> Cockney
> Yank

Can you add any more to this list?
In pairs, guess or find out which area is referred to in each case, and discuss the reasons why you think each is used. On which occasions might each name be considered either a compliment or an insult? Are the terms used equally of men and women?

Does accent matter?

Do you think that some accents sound better than others? Surveys have shown that people prefer the sound of certain accents to others. Can you guess which these might be? To see what members of your class think, follow this exercise:

1. Make a class list of *ten* well-known accents.
2. In pairs, rank these accents in order of merit, from 1 to 10. To do this, you will need to agree on what you mean by *merit*. Attractiveness? Intelligence?
3. Join another pair and compare the ratings you have given each accent. See whether you can agree on a group rating.
4. Now explain your group ratings to the class.

Can you explain why some accents are considered better than others? How just is this, in your view?

Accents in the media

How does the media portray accents? In groups, think of TV or radio programmes that rely on regional/social class accents for effect.

> soap operas
>
> quiz and game shows
>
> comedy serials and shows
>
> adverts

What is the importance of the accents in each case? What impression do they give of people who speak in these ways?

These phrases are from a guide to the Lancashire dialect entitled *Lanky Spoken Here*:

Visiting the Doctor

Are theaw't quack?
Excuse me, are you the doctor?

Ah feel wake
I feel weak

Ah keep gooin' mazey
I am continually having dizzy spells

Ah'm aw cowd crills
I am shivering

Ah varnear collopst
I have nearly collapsed

Ah'm reet jiggered
I am tired out through effort

Ah'm cowfin lahk a good-un
I can't seem to stop coughing

Ah'm powfagged
I'm weary/browbeaten

Ah'm too double wi't bellywarch
I'm doubled up with stomach pains

Ah've getten yedwarch
My head aches

Ah'm bun up
I am constipated
(egg-bun is the state of being constipated through eating too many eggs)

Ah cud do wi summat purra road through me
Please prescribe me a laxative
(also known as **oppenin'-medicine**)

Mi guts're off
I have tummy trouble

Cough it up – it met be a pianner
Get it off your chest (phlegm)

Ees ta'n bad roads
The patient is getting worse

Ah'm still a bit tickle
I am still not quite right

Ah've a spile in mi ont
I have a splinter in my hand

Ah've summat in mi een
I have something in my eye

Ah feel lahk am on feigher
I am running a temperature

Ah think ahm mendin'
I am getting much better

It's chickinpots
Chickenpox

It's summat an' nowt
You'll survive

Ah'm swettin' lahk a pig
I have a perspiration problem

Purruz on't club wilta?
I wish to receive National Health benefits

Ah'm up stick
I think I am pregnant

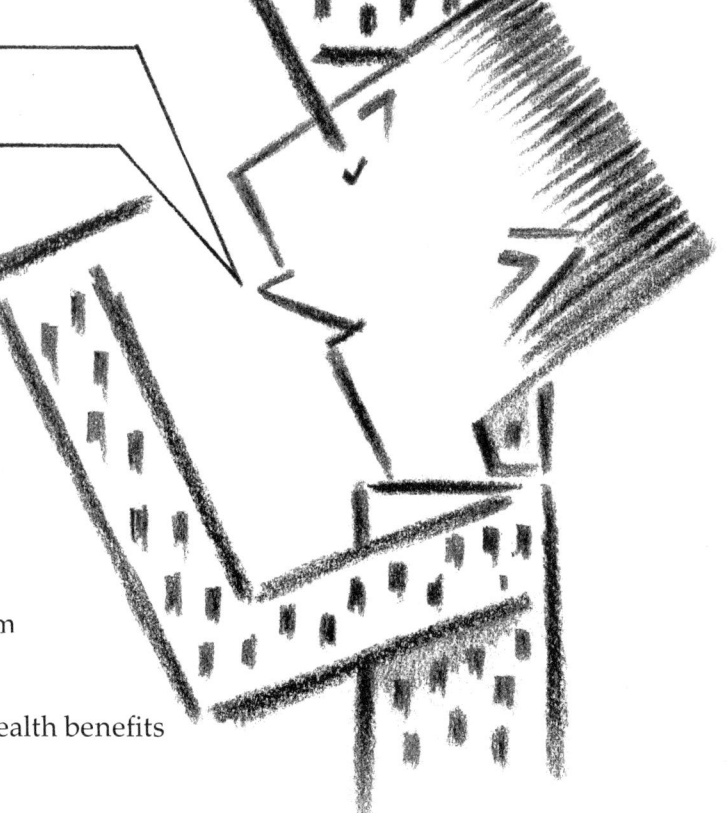

M. & J. Hobbs

This poem, menu and drawing are all from a guide to Cockney dialect and slang:

Uncle George

Me old Uncle George was a shuvver.
Gawd! 'e 'ad the gift o' the gab,
'e'd go on 'arf the night
(If 'e wasn't too tight)
To the geezers 'e drove in 'is cab.

Baht the 'ard-up and 'ungery firties
When a bloke 'ud damn near sell 'is soul
To any old Nob
Wot 'ud give 'im a job
And save 'im from takin' the dole.

Yer couldn't afford to be choosy,
Yer'd work 'till yer dropped for a quid
Fer yer trouble and strife
And to keep bref o' life
In a couple o' young saucepan lids.

There wasn't no trips to Majorca
Wiv good bees and 'oney to spend.
Yer'd be living it 'igh
Wiv two bob in yer sky
On a charrybang bahnd for Sahfend.

If old Uncle could put up for parlement
'ed stand on 'is plates and 'ed shaht,
In a voice full o' scorn,
"Lads, yer dun-no yer born,
Yer dun-no wot 'ardship's abaht.

"Nah take a perfunctory butchers
At our standard o' living today,
We've all got a telly,
A full derby kelly –
And we're striking the 'ol lot away!

"Britannia's gawn right up the Swanee,
Wiv closed minces we foller the oafs.
It's a bad two and eight;
Buckle to, me ol' mates,
And for crying aht lahd use yer loafs!"

Barbara Hoy

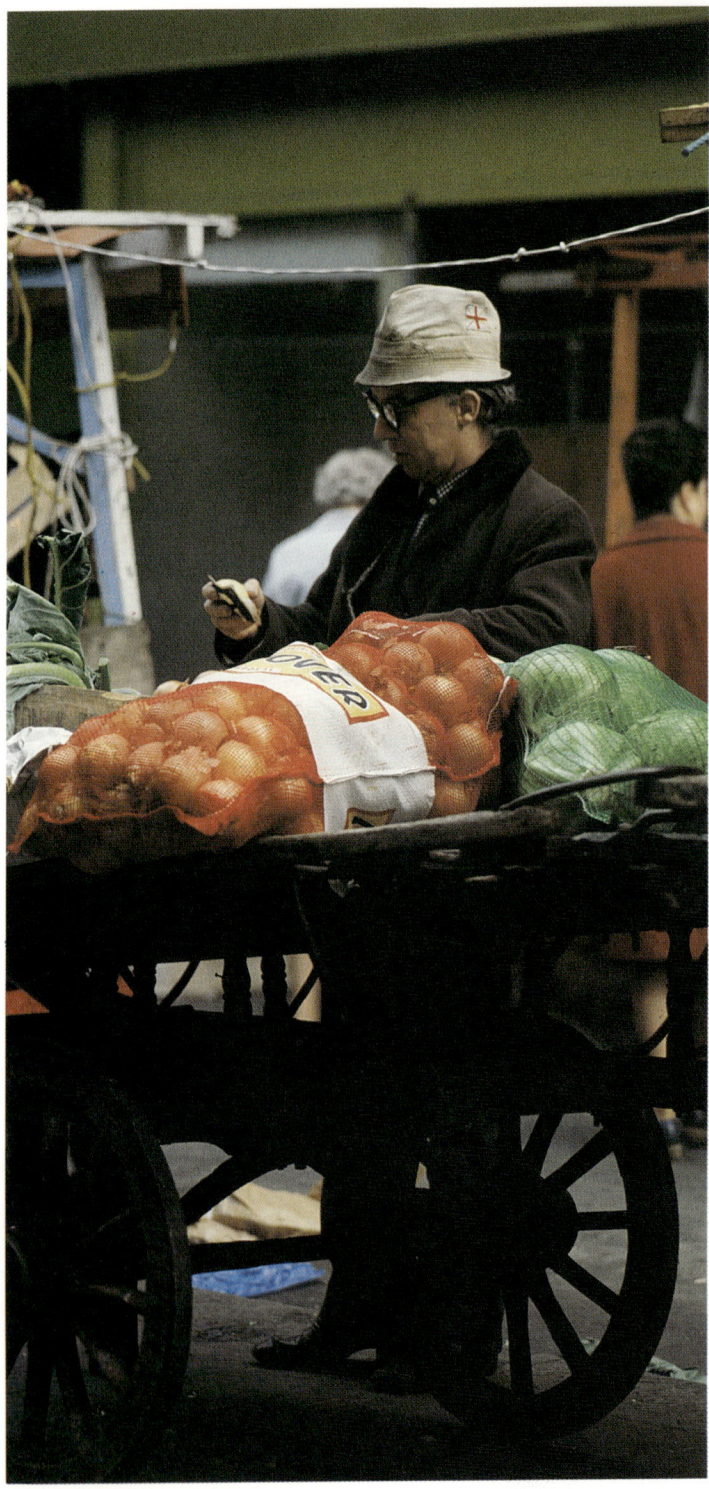

NOSH

Relish
jellied *ee-uz* (eels), winkles
or salad with *crease* (cress)

Main course
faggot stoo (stew), with *saveloys* and *spuds*

Afters
dish of custard
appuz (apples), *goosegogs* (gooseberries)
an' *cracker-nuts* (hazel nuts)

To sup
cuppa Rosie wiv a dollop o' sugar,
worth draining to the *grahts* (dregs)
or a *pint o' pig's ear* (beer)

CLOTHES

- titfer (tat)
- 'alf a dollar
- Dicky Dirt
- Peckham Rye
- Epsom races
- Dover boat, all afloat, isle afloat (coat)
- Sky rocket, Lucy Locket
- rahnd de 'ahses (trousers) rank an' riches (breeches)
- almond rocks, Katharine Docks
- daisy roots

ALSO
Bryant an' Mays 'stays'
(from the match manufacturers)

Irish jig 'wig'

Jack the Ripper 'slippers'

okey-doke 'poke, pocket'
(old word as in 'a pig in a poke')

steam-packet 'jacket'

these an' those 'clothes'

turtle doves 'gloves'

watercressed 'dressed'

whistle an' flute 'suit'

Yorkshire blues 'shoes'

Both Liz Lochhead and Tom Leonard write here in their native Glaswegian dialect:

Favourite Shade
(Rap)

She's getting No More Black, her.
You've got bugger all bar black, Barbra.
Black's dead drab an' all.
Ah'd never have been seen
deid in it, your age tae!
Dreich. As a shade it's draining.
Better aff
somethin tae pit a bit a colour in her cheeks,
 eh no?
Black. Hale wardrobe fulla black claes.
Jist hingin' therr half the time, emmty.
On the hangers, hingin.
Plus by the way a gloryhole
Chockablock with bermuda shorts, the lot.
Yella Kimono, ah don't know
whit all.
Tropical prints.
Polyester everything Easy-Kerr. Bit naw, naw
that was last year, noo
she's no one to give
nothing coloured
houseroom. Black. Black.
Ah'm fed up tae the back teeth lukkin' ett her.
Feyther says the same.

Who's peyin' fur it onlywey?
Wance yir workin' weer whit yi like.
No as if yiv nothin' tae pit oan yir back.
Black!
As well oot the world as oot the fashion.

Seen a wee skirt in Miss Selfridge.
Sort of dove, it was lovely.
Would she weer it, but?
Goes: see if it was black
it'd be brilliant.

Liz Lochhead

The Dropout

scrimpt nscraipt furryi
urryi grateful
no wan bit

speylt useless yi urr
twistid izza coarkscrew
cawz rowz inan empty hooss

yir fathir nivirid yoor chance
pick n choozyir joab
a steady pey

well jiss take a lookit yirsell
naithur wurk nur wahnt
aw aye

yir clivir
damm clivir
but yi huvny a clue whutyir dayn

Tom Leonard

This poem, written in Afro-Caribbean English, is influenced by the sounds of Reggae music. It is best read aloud:

De Youths

Dem youths now a days
dem no skin up no way
dem jus a trod it inna
militant style

Some sport fashion
on social security rations
dem no care how dem
walk dem jus wile

For is style dem a check
not de YTS set
dem a walk an a show
nuff coil

dem a break dance
dem a robot
dem a move wid de
up town groove

dem a lyric chatter
an a wise cracker
dem jus a bob
an a weave
an a move

De youth man dem
chat bout girl frien
an how dem control
up dem worl
but de youth women
say dem an dem a no frien

For is big mistake
youth man a make
if dem tink de daughter
a bow

For de youth women
wicked and wile
always drop it inna a warrior
style

always de in dem own possie
Thru youth man
gwan bossie
dem no scared a treat
cause when dem get vex
dem prepared to put up a fight

So our youth people
a no simple people
dem jus need a positive guide
for when culture
come and dem dash whey
dem fun
dem will come wid a wickeda style

Nefertiti Gayle

D. H. Lawrence wrote in both his native Nottinghamshire dialect and in Standard English:

A Collier's Wife

Somebody's knocking at the door
    Mother, come down and see.
– I's think it's nobbut a beggar,
    Say, I'm busy.

It's not a beggar, mother, – hark
    How hard he knocks...
– Eh, tha'rt a mard-'arsed kid,
    'E'll gi'e thee socks!

Shout an' ax what 'e wants,
    I canna come down.
– 'E says 'Is it Arthur Holliday's?'
    Say 'Yes,' tha clown.

'E says, 'Tell your mother as 'er mester's
    Got hurt i' th' pit.'
What – oh my sirs, 'e never says that,
    That's niver it.

Come out o' the way an' let me see,
    Eh, there's no peace!
An' stop thy scraightin', childt,
    Do shut thy face.

'Your mester's 'ad an accident,
    An' they're ta'ein 'im i' th' ambulance
To Nottingham,' – Eh dear o' me
    If 'e's not a man for mischance!

Wheers he hurt this time, lad?
    – I dunna know,
They on'y towd me it wor bad –
    It would be so!

Eh, what a man! – an' that cobbly road,
    They'll jolt him a'most to death,
I'm sure he's in for some trouble
    Nigh every time he takes breath.

Out o' my way, childt – dear o' me, wheer
    Have I put his clean stockings and shirt;
Goodness knows if they'll be able
    To take off his pit dirt.

An' what a moan he'll make – there niver
    Was such a man for a fuss
If anything ailed him – at any rate
    I shan't have him to nuss.

I do hope it's not very bad!
    Eh, what a shame it seems
As some should ha'e hardly a smite o' trouble
    An' others has reams.

It's a shame as 'e should be knocked about
    Like this, I'm sure it is!
He's had twenty accidents, if he's had one;
    Owt bad, an' it's his.

There's one thing, we'll have peace for a bit,
    Thank Heaven for a peaceful house;
An' there's compensation, sin' it's accident,
    An' club money – I nedn't grouse.

An' a fork an' a spoon he'll want, an' what else;
    I s'll never catch that train –
What a traipse it is if a man gets hurt –
    I s'd think he'll get right again.

D. H. Lawrence

The Oxford Voice

When you hear it languishing
and hooing and cooing and sidling through the front teeth,
      the Oxford voice
      or worse still
      the would-be-Oxford voice
you don't even laugh any more, you can't.

For every blooming bird is an Oxford cuckoo nowadays,
you can't sit on a bus nor in the tube
but it breathes gently and languishingly in the back of your
    neck.

And oh, so seductively superior, so seductively
        self-effacingly
        deprecatingly
        superior.

We wouldn't insist on it for a moment
        but we are
        we are
        you admit we are
        superior.

D. H. Lawrence

ACTIVITIES

Please read the glossary on p.66 before starting these Activities.

Reading aloud

In groups of three or four, choose *one* of the following:

- *Uncle George*
- **both** *The Dropout* **and** *Favourite Shade*
- *A Collier's Wife*
- *De Youths*

Together work out a reading of your chosen poem. Experiment with the way you read it, for example:
– each person, in turn, reads a stanza,
– chosen words, phrases or lines in each stanza are read in chorus,
– speech is read by one voice; narrative by another.

When you have practised your reading, perform it to the class or make a tape-recording of it.

A glossary

Make a glossary of the poem your group has chosen in the activity above. If you have problems with 'translating' particular words, try:
making a guess; checking with other people; finding a dialect handbook in your library. Here is how you might begin to chart your glossary of the dialect words in *Uncle George*:

Take the first two stanzas of the poem you have glossed. 'Translate' these stanzas into Standard English.
- Is anything gained by translating the verse?
- What do you feel is lost in the translation?
- How important is it for this poem to be in dialect?

Cockney English	Standard English
shuvver	chauffeur
Gawd	
gift o' the gab	
e'd	he would
go on	
	half
tight	

A dialect phrase book

Write a chapter for a dialect phrase book to be used by visitors to your area. To help you, look at a foreign language phrase book, and use the chapter from *Lanky Spoken Here* and look at the Cockney menu and guide to clothes on p.59. Your phrase book should list common expressions and show how these are pronounced. It may also include diagrams. Here are some ideas for chapters:

> Eating out
> Visiting the doctor
>   dentist
>   hairdresser
>   police station
> Sightseeing
> In your hotel
> Going shopping
>   buying food
>   clothes etc,
> Repairing your car
> Entertainments

Scriptwriters' meeting

In groups of up to six, choose a soap opera which you all enjoy, and imagine that you are its team of scriptwriters. Prepare to write part of an episode which you predict might happen in a few weeks time. (Each person might take responsibility for a particular scene, or for a group of characters.) To help you, watch an episode of the programme, listening carefully to the use of dialect. Take particular note of:

- expressions and vocabulary in common use by all the characters,
- the way individual characters typically speak.

When each of you has written your scene(s), hold a second scriptwriters' meeting. Read out your contribution and ask the others to comment on how accurate your use of dialect is. When you have edited your scripts, and agreed on a 'running order', try a group reading of the episode. This will be to ensure that the scripts are ready to pass on to the actors.

A dialect poem

Choose one poem you particularly like from the selection in this chapter. Write a poem of your own using the same dialect and style as your chosen poem. It may help if the class can generate some ideas for titles of poems, in the same way as these examples:

> **Liz Lochhead**
> 'Favourite music
>   food
>   hairstyle
>   footwear
>   etc'
>
> **Nefertiti Gayle**
> 'De Old People'
> 'De Workers'
> 'De Youth Women'
>
> **D. H. Lawrence**
> 'The BBC Voice'
> 'Down Pit'
> 'Her Husband'

Living English

English is alive – it is always changing. Every day the language acquires new words, for example, from computer technology or from other languages. Gradually English loses old words which are no longer useful. English also varies from place to place. People who come from a particular place speak in a distinctive way. Here is a glossary of terms which describe living English:

Accent – the way words are pronounced, usually in a certain region but sometimes associated with social class. For example:
I wer in t' West Marshes wi't' gun, when I wer hoping for a rabbit burra nivver seed nowt all day. **(Yorkshire accent)**
I jess dono watser matter, Bruce, I jess got no ebb tide these dyes. **(Australian accent)**

Dialect – a distinctive form of language usually from a particular region. Speaking in a local dialect affects accent, use of grammar and choice of expressions. For example:
I ain' got no dough to give yer. **(Cockney dialect)**
Tha' niver said thankyer for nowt i' thy life, did ter? **(Nottinghamshire dialect)**

Received pronunciation – the accent of spoken British English which is understood throughout the world. Frequently used in education and broadcasting. Sometimes known as 'BBC accent' or 'Southern accent' or simply, 'posh'!

Standard English – the dialect of English officially used throughout the world for writing and printed materials. It has an established grammar, punctuation and spelling. School coursework is supposed to be written in Standard English. However, it may be spoken with a local accent.

Colloquial language – chatty language used only in speech and not usually considered appropriate in written English. For example:
I felt shattered, so I crashed out on the sofa.

Slang – a more extreme version of colloquial language, often more vulgar and humorous. For example:
I'm going out with that cool bird you fancy.
I murdered a pint then stuffed my face with chips!

Register – The form of language you choose to use in different situations. For example: local dialect and slang to a friend; Standard English at a job interview; technical English to a computer programmer; baby talk to a new-born.

If you were to write down the way you actually sound when you speak, it would not look much like Standard written English, whoever you are. Try this sentence in pairs, with one person saying it and the other writing down the exact sounds:

Mike's father has bought this great new house in Spain.

Now swap over. Have you both written the sentence down in the same way? If not, why might this be?

In pairs, take this conversation in standard spelling and 'translate' it into any dialect you both know. Change any words or phrases to fit this dialect. Then practise it using the appropriate accent:

Hello. How are you? Are you coming out tonight?
  Sorry, no, I can't. I've got no money.
Look, are you my friend or not?
  I can't keep borrowing money from you.
Don't be an idiot. We can just go and sit on the park bench.
  Oh good idea. I think I'll stay at home.

See if you can add more slang words/phrases to this list:

Money: dough, greens, readies...
Idiot: twit, burk, nit...
Good: ace, neat, cool...
Happy: over the moon, A1...
Sad: blue, down in the dumps...

Now try slang expressions for police, friend, food, dying/death, clothes.

Do you know any Cockney rhyming slang? For example *use your loaf* comes from the rhyming slang *loaf of bread* (head). List any examples you know. Look for further examples of rhyming slang on pp.58-59.

In pairs, act out how you would greet and begin a conversation with: A school friend
Your doctor
The Queen
A younger brother or sister
Your mum/dad.

6 · Using dialogue

STARTERS

One liners

In pairs, continue a conversation between you starting with one of the lines below:

> 'Well, someone's got to tell him...'
> 'You can't come in here dressed like that...'
> 'Excuse me, but you've just dropped this...'
> 'Look, I've got something to tell you...'
> 'Have you been waiting here long?'
> 'I've never seen you before in my life...'

Provoking comments

What do you say when you want to provoke a parent or an adult?

> 'All my friends' parents...'
> 'You're mean!'
> 'You never let me...'

See if your group can add to this list.

The generation gap

Still in pairs, look at the picture on the left-hand page. Imagine an old lady walks past a youth in a shopping precinct and a conversation begins like this:

> 'Disgrace... hair just like a bird's nest...'
> 'You talking to me, grandma?...'

The old lady takes up the challenge. Continue the conversation between the old lady and the youth. If you like, work in groups, adding other roles to your sketch – friends of the youth, or a police officer.

Conversation diary

Keep a diary for a single day – from early morning to bedtime – in which you record all the main conversations you have with people. You might make your notes under such headings as:

> Time
> With whom?
> Subject
> Purpose
> Mood/tone

After writing your diary, discuss in groups what you have written. What are the similarities and differences in the ways each of you converse?

Keeping the Lines of Communication open

Posy Simmonds, The Guardian

Teenagerspeak is from *The Extremely Serious Guide To Parenthood*. The left-hand column gives examples of typical teenage speech. The right-hand column gives the real meaning, according to Keith Ray.

Teenagerspeak

'Is it all right if I ask a friend round?'	'Is it all right if I ask a couple of dozen friends round?'
'Is it all right if I ask a few friends round?'	'We're going to have a party, and we want to have it here.'
'Are you going out tonight?'	'We don't want you around for the party because we'll all be getting drunk and worse... and I wasn't planning to tell you about the party in any case.'
'I won't stay out late.'	'You might see me before breakfast.'
'It's one of those feminine problems you wouldn't understand' (said to a father by a daughter).	'I'm going to play my trump card.'
'It's one of those feminine problems you wouldn't understand' (said by a son to a father).	'I'm going to tell you something that'll get you *really* worried.'
'You're being so old-fashioned / fuddy-duddy / square, etc.' (a real thrust to the jugular, this one).	'You're right, but if I capitalise on your vanity there's just a slight chance I might get away with it.'
'If *you* can do it then why can't I?'	Get out of *that* one if you can.

Keith Ray

This complete scene is taken from a play devised by a group of young women playwrights for the Second Wave Festival. It is intended either to be read aloud, or performed on stage.

A Netful of Holes

ANDREA LEAVING HOME

Andrea arrives home as usual. Her mother is cooking the dinner.

Andrea Evening Mum.
Mum Hallo. Go see to the meat. Had a good day?
Andrea Mum?
Mum Yes dear.
Andrea Can I talk to you?
Mum Are you working tomorrow?
Andrea I want to leave home.
Mum (*ignores this*) Don't let that meat burn.
Andrea Mum?
Mum What.
Andrea I'm thinking of leaving home.
Mum What!
Andrea I'm thinking of leaving home.
Mum WHAT!!!
Andrea I want to be independent.
Mum You are independent. You live your own life. I don't trouble you when you come in, you go out. I don't ask where you're coming from, where you're going.
Andrea That's not what it is.
Mum I don't understand . . .
Andrea I'm moving out. I'm moving in with a friend.
Mum Moving? When?
Andrea Next couple of days.
Mum Next couple of days. What friend? So you can go rub-a-dub and ting with that boy you met last week? Is it so? No. You're not moving out. You stay in that chair. You're eighteen years of age, you left school last month and you find yourself a job and now you want to leave?
Andrea I'm leaving.
Mum No.
Andrea You can't stop me.
Mum I can.

Andrea You can't stop me going out that door and not coming back.
Mum You been thinking about it?
Andrea Yes. I want to live my *own* life.
Mum You live your own life.
Andrea I want to make my own mistakes, to be a woman, a free woman.
Mum My God, what is she saying to me?
Andrea What you said round the table, about wanting to be free, when you were young. Remember? You were the same age as me, Mum, you can't have forgotten.
Mum No child. I've not forgotten. I haven't forgotten how hard it was, how painful. Andrea, that big blasted world doesn't care. *I care!*
Andrea I know Mum, I know all that. It's different now. I've got a place, it's big enough for the two of us. I've got money and a job. You've taught me how to look after myself. I feel so good about this, excited . . . you've *got* to understand.
Mum There are some bad people out there. Bad, bad, bad.
Andrea Listen to me. I'm not going on to the streets.
Mum You're not going nowhere.
Andrea God, you make me mad.
Mum You're all I've got.
Andrea I've made up my mind.
Mum Why Good Lord? (*she breaks down*)
Andrea Shut up, Mum. Look. Don't cry. (*moves to touch her*)
Mum Get off me. Girl you have a lot to learn. I brought you up. I put clothes on your back and food in your belly. This is what I get. Stupid selfish child.
Andrea My bags are packed. I'm leaving the day after tomorrow. I'm going to live with Ali.
Mum Who's this Ali?
Andrea She's okay. She's older . . .

Mum It's not funny. You'll get nothing out of me once you leave.

Knock at the door

Mum Who's that?
Andrea It's her. We were going to show you the flat.
Mum Let her in... I got some things to say to her!
Andrea Mum I'm warning you, don't start.
Mum Let the girl in.

Andrea goes to the front door. Re-enter Andrea with Ali

Ali (*ignoring Mum, to Andrea*) Are you ready? My boyfriend's waiting in the car.
Mum What's your name... Alley cat?
Andrea (*to Mum*) You make me sick you do.
Mum (*to Ali*) So where is this place of yours?
Ali Not far.
Mum (*to Andrea*) If you think you're moving in with *her*...! (*to Ali*) You're not leaving with *my* daughter!
Ali I'm not forcing her.
Mum Who do you think you are? Talking to me like that.
Andrea Mum. If you don't stop, I'm walking out. (*to Ali*) Take no notice.
Ali Do you want to see the flat, Mrs Martin?
Mum I'm not going nowhere.
Andrea Mum. Come on. Come with us.
Mum No.

Ali Come on. They're waiting.
Mum They can wait. (*to Ali*) Now just get this straight... this is *my* daughter.
Andrea Ten out of ten for observation.
Ali (*to Andrea*) Shush. I understand how you feel Mrs Martin.
Mum You? Understand how I feel? Have you children, child?
Ali No.
Mum Have you ever known what it was like to bring up a young child in a strange country? All on your own. No support, people attacking you on the street, calling you names, on your hands and knees cleaning up after filthy people, people that treat you like dirt.
Ali (*interrupting*) You know I haven't Mrs Martin.
Mum *I* have. And sometimes the only thing that kept me alive was my daughter.
Ali Please Mrs Martin. Things are different now. (*pause*) Why don't you come see the place?
Mum No. I'm tired. I'm staying at home. *My* home.
Ali I'm going now. (*aside*) See you downstairs Andrea. (*leaves*)
Andrea Mum. *Please* try to understand.
Mum I'll try, but I don't think I will.
Andrea For God's sake. It's only down the road.
Mum It's not here.

The title and the ending (about 120 words in length), have been removed from this short story:

The table had a formica top to it – a dubious mottled pink punctuated with cigarette burns. A green aluminium ashtray, quietly choking on cigarette ends, an untouched bar of chocolate, a battered copy of *Gone with the Wind* and a tube of antiseptic cream – half-used – distinguished the table from the ten or so others in the antiseptic room. And three pairs of elbows. The three pairs of eyes belonging to the three pairs of elbows bored a hole in the expiring ashtray.

'You are still taking your pills though, dear?'

'Yes, Mother.'

'Because you must take them you know.'

'I know, Mother.'

'Your pills.'

'Mother, I am still taking my pills. I am taking my pills with a vengeance. I am putting all the energy, all the youthful vigour of my twenty-one years into taking my pills. I am taking the taking of my pills very seriously, Mother.'

'There's no need to talk to your mother like that, Neil', said his father, evenly.

'No, there's no need to talk to me like that, Neil,' said his mother.

Silence reasserted itself again, pressing the elbows into the table, the eyes into the ashtray. Slices of conversations found their way across the room from the other tables. Mrs Pritchard's bunions, apparently, were no better, it must be her time of life, Chelsea hadn't deserved to win the FA Cup in 1970, load of fairies anyway, someone hoped someone else liked carnations, and didn't they match the tables perfectly how nice, it's the darkness, yes, the garden's lovely.

'The Vicar sends his love and blessings, Neil,' his mother remembered. 'And I saw Mark the other day outside the butcher's, he says he'll try and come along sometime next week to see you.'

'Mark?'

'Yes, dear – it is Mark, isn't it?'

'Mike, Mother, Mike, I know no one called Mark, Mike you mean.'

'Yes, dear – the boy with the large buttocks.

'You have an unerring eye for detail, Mother.

Neil's father lit a cigarette. In his large, powerful hand the white cylinder looked curiously insubstantial, almost vulnerable. Neil waited for the words to come – the lawn or the dog?

'The lawn's looking marvellous, anyway. Mum and I have had a good go at it this weekend.'

The lawn. Of course the lawn.

'We wanted to get the garden looking nice for next week when you come home,' his mother almost apologized.

Searching for a reply, Neil shifted his elbows on the formica, picked up the chocolate between his finger and thumb, balanced it upright on the paperback – thus obscuring Clark Gable's nose and half his face, an improvement, he thought – and became acutely interested in the tinfoil wrapping. 'Yes, it's nice when the lawn is nice,' he managed. This observation seemed agreeable to all.

'Tea?' a voice threatened. And again, louder this time: 'Tea?' A trolley rumbled and clanked its way in a slightly wounded fashion across the linoleum, attached to a woman in a pink overall and very low-heeled shoes. China wobbled.

'It's coming this way,' thought Neil, and started to study the screw-on cap of the tube of antiseptic cream as his mother began to smile in a general manner.

'Tea?'

'Tea, Neil!' exclaimed his mother, attempting to suggest surprised delight, as if the trolley and its accomplice were a new invention. 'Would you like some tea? Yes, let's have some tea, thank you very much, we'd love some.'

The tea was deposited rather than poured into three anonymous white china cups and the trolley lurched off.

They sipped.

Eventually: 'Dr Anderson said you were almost ready to come out this week, Neil,' said his father, 'but we all agreed it was best for you to stay the extra week.'

'To make sure you're quite recovered,' clarified his mother.

'Yes, to make sure you're quite recovered. You mustn't rush these things. He seems a very reasonable bloke to me, this Dr Anderson?'

'He stinks,' said Neil, with heavy precision.

'Neil!' his mother exclaimed, looking about her whilst trying to reassemble her general smile, 'how dare you speak like that about Dr Anderson who's helped you so much. You've always been so rude!' And then in case this last sentence had been loud enough to catch the ears of another table: 'Fruit and nut is your favourite, isn't it?'

Neil said, 'Yes it is. Thank you very much.' And meant it.

The ashtray again.

Chairs started to complain on the linoleum, handbags clipped shut, keys jingled as the other visitors started to take their leave. See you next week then, and the roses of course, love to Jack, no, it was last Tuesday, well then. Slowly the rest of the pink formica reassumed control of the room.

'Well then,' Neil's father suggested.

'We must be off now, Neil,' said his mother, confidentially. 'Now you will take your pills like Dr Anderson said?'

'Yes, Mother.'

'And not flush them down the toilet again?'

'No, Mother.'

'And do get enough sleep, dear.'

'I shall, Mother.'

They got up, as one. Neil's father held out one statuesque hand. Neil shook it, in silence.

'Is there anything else you want, then?'

Jonathan Steffan

Teenagerspeak/Parentspeak

Read *Teenagerspeak* on p.71. In pairs, work out a similar list of *Parentspeak*. To get you started, look at these examples:

'I won't tell you again!' 　'I won't tell you again until next time I tell you.'

'Go to bed now, you need sleep.' 　'Go to bed now . . . we need a break from you.'

In pairs, work out a dialogue in 'double talk' between a teenager and an adult. Set it out in playscript form, but use a double column – the left side for what is said aloud, and the right side for the real meaning. Choose one of these subjects for your dialogue:

- time to go to bed
- an untidy bedroom
- going out
- eating the meal
- having a friend (or two) round
- watching television

Now work with another pair and play each scene with four actors. For this use the *thought-tracking* convention: two actors play each part – one speaking the words, the other speaking the thoughts. (See p.**198**.)

Shock announcement

Read the scene from *A Netful of Holes* either as a class, or in groups. Then discuss the answers to these questions:

- What do you think of the way Andrea prepares her mother for the news that she is leaving home?
- Could she have avoided the confrontation with her mother, and the unhappiness she causes?

In pairs or threes, work out a role play involving two to four characters, which is triggered by a shock announcement. Decide whether you go for a confrontation which ends badly, or whether you allow your characters to resolve the problem in a dignified way. Choose one of these lines, or one of your own:

'I've got a bad report.'
'I've failed all my exams.'
'My bike was stolen at school today.'
'I want to go on holiday with my boy/girlfriend's family this year.'
'Can I have £200 to go on a skiing holiday with the school?'
'Look what I've spent your birthday money on . . .'
'I don't want to stay on at school.'
'I've brought home a pet . . . it was going to be put down . . .'

When you have worked out a dialogue, decide whether you will give a 'live' performance to the class, or make a tape-recording of it.

Predicting the story

Read the story without a title (on pp.74-75) at least twice before discussing these questions in pairs:

- What kind of place is Neil in, and how do you know this?
- Why do you think he is there?
- Why might he have flushed the pills away?
- Who do you have more sympathy for; Neil or his parents? Why do you feel like this?

Still in pairs, discuss your ideas for the following:

A title

Brainstorm a list of at least ten titles for this story. Then discuss which are the best three or so, rejecting the rest. Choose a title for the story from your shortlist, justifying why you have chosen this one and rejected the other two.

An ending

How do you imagine this story might end? Still working in pairs, draft two alternative endings for the story, each to be about 120 words long. Use a style of writing similar to the original – that is, a mixture of dialogue and narrative. Choose your two endings from this list of types:

unexpected, surprise or shock, depressing, hopeful, humorous, 'circular' i.e. finishing in a similar way to the beginning.

Story follow-on

Write a follow-on to the story of Neil and his parents, based on one of these approaches, or on an idea of your own:

1. Neil meets Dr Anderson for a consultation, shortly before he is due home. The doctor is trying to prepare Neil for the outside world, and particularly for living with his parents again. Neil is determined to be uncooperative...

2. Dr Anderson meets Neil and his parents for the last time before he is discharged. Neil's parents are trying hard to be positive about the future but Neil is still behaving in a disturbing way...

In your choice of story follow-on, aim to show how strained the conversation is, and what people's real thoughts might be. You can suggest the strain in the dialogue itself, but also by describing the actions and voice tones of the characters.

TECHNIQUES

Using dialogue

The exercises in this section are linked with the extract from *A Netful of Holes*.

When you use dialogue in role play, it helps you to understand your own feelings and experiences. It will also help you to identify with other people's. When you read, dialogue can strengthen your belief and involvement in a text. This is because it has at least three functions:

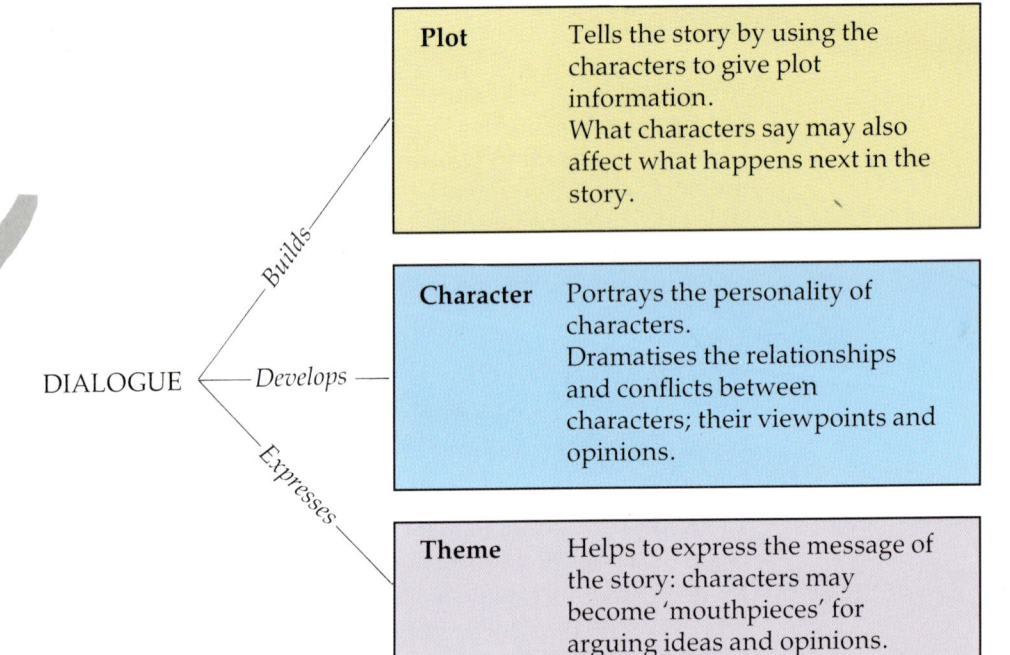

DIALOGUE
- *Builds* → **Plot**: Tells the story by using the characters to give plot information. What characters say may also affect what happens next in the story.
- *Develops* → **Character**: Portrays the personality of characters. Dramatises the relationships and conflicts between characters; their viewpoints and opinions.
- *Expresses* → **Theme**: Helps to express the message of the story: characters may become 'mouthpieces' for arguing ideas and opinions.

- In drama, we learn about the plot or storyline from the dialogue between the characters. See if you can summarise (in about 40 words) the main storyline in the scene from *A Netful of Holes*.
- Write a brief description (less than 100 words), of Andrea's character for an actress who will be taking her part. How much information is provided by the playscript? How much is left open to interpretation?
- 'The message of *A Netful of Holes* is...'
Complete this sentence using your own words to describe the main message, or viewpoint of the scene. How does your summary compare with a partner's?

Make it natural

Try to write dialogue in the way that people really speak. Draw your dialogue from real life and your experience of the way people speak. The role plays you perform in class will help you to write dialogue. Remember, the test of a good dialogue is whether it works when you read it aloud!

Make it dynamic

Dialogue in writing is often used to express conflict. So use short speeches and make sure your characters are reacting to each other. Where appropriate, make your dialogue lively and energetic. In the short story on pp.74-75, the dialogue is intended to be flat and strained – but the writer deliberately mixes polite 'small talk' with violent outbursts.

Give it a purpose

Plan your dialogue beforehand. Decide what you wish to express. Do you wish to: tell a story; show clashes between characters; convey a message; get a response from your reader such as laughter or shock?

Make it true to character

If you want to portray a minor character in dialogue, you can suggest this in various simple ways – a certain accent or dialect, typical expressions, a repeated viewpoint and so on. Try to avoid crude *stereotypes* which people know are not 'real'.

If you want to portray a main character, use dialogue which shows how complex, unpredictable and distinctive people can be. Their speech may include everyday conversation, fierce argument and rich reflection.

> Remember that whether you are portraying a minor or main character, s/he may sometimes behave in *stereotyped* ways and sometimes not. For example, an old lady may moan about youth today and talk nostalgically about the past, but still enjoy the company of young people and wish to learn from them.

7 · Expressing my thoughts

My thoughts

I sometimes wonder what my mind is like inside, often I fancy that it is like this. I feel as if my mind goes round and round like the earth and if my lessons make me think hard it begins to spin. In my other class it was getting all stodgy and still and lumpy and rusty. I feel as if there is a ball in my mind and it is divided into pieces – each piece stands for a different mood. The ball turns every now and then and that's what makes me change moods. I have my learning mood, my goodlooks mood, my happy mood, my loose-end mood and my grumpy mood, my missrable mood, my thoughtful mood and my planning mood. At the moment I am writing this I am in my thoughtful mood. When I am in my thoughtful mood I think out my maths and plan stories and poems. When my kitten is in her thoughtful mood she thinks shall I pounce or not, and shall I go to sleep or not. This sort of thing goes on in my own mind too. It is very hard for me to put my thoughts into words.

Sarah Gristwood, aged 7

Thoughts in my head

How are your own views of the world formed? Directly from your own head? From contact with other people?
Draw a diagram like this one with connecting lines to all the sources you believe your ideas come from:

Which source is the most important, and which the least? Do you think that any of these sources might prevent you from thinking more freely?

In ten years' time

How do you see your life in ten years' time? In pairs, discuss what you might both be doing. Think of: work, home life, relationships, family, your hopes and ambitions, the society you will live in – better or worse?

Caged or free?

In groups, think of all the ways in which you are *free* in your life. Think of your position at home and at school, as well as your position in society. You might compare your position with people living in other countries, where certain freedoms are not taken for granted. Then, make a group list beginning:

> 'We are free to . . .'

Now make a list of all the ways in which you are *not* free in your life. Again make a group list, this time beginning:

> 'We are not free to . . .'

On balance, does freedom outweigh lack of freedom when you compare the two lists?

After this activity, you might consider drawing up a Young People's Charter – your own declaration of the rights and freedoms to which all young people should be entitled.

Martin Luther King was an American civil rights leader who fought hard against 'the triple evils' of racism, poverty and war. This, his most famous speech, was given in 1963, to a mass rally of 250,000 people in Washington DC, who were demanding full integration of blacks in American society. In 1968, he was assassinated by a sniper as he stood talking on a hotel balcony in Memphis, Tennessee.

"I Have a Dream"

...I say to you today, my friends, that in spite of the difficulties and frustrations of the moment I still have a dream. It is a dream deeply rooted in the American dream.

I have a dream that one day this nation will rise up and live out the true meaning of its creed. "We hold these truths to be self-evident; that all men are created equal."

I have a dream that one day on the red hills of Georgia the sons of former slaves and the sons of former slaveowners will be able to sit down together at the table of brotherhood.

I have a dream that one day even the state of Mississippi, a desert state sweltering with the heat of injustice and oppression, will be transformed into an oasis of freedom and justice.

I have a dream that my four little children will one day live in a nation where they will not be judged by the color of their skin but by the content of their character.

I have a dream today.

I have a dream that one day the state of Alabama, whose governor's lips are presently dripping with the words of interposition and nullification, will be transformed into a situation where little black boys and black girls will be able to join hands with little white boys and white girls and walk together as sisters and brothers.

I have a dream today.

I have a dream that one day every valley shall be exalted, every hill and mountain shall be made low, the rough places will be made plains, and the crooked places will be made straight, and the glory of the Lord shall be revealed, and all flesh shall see it together.

This is our hope. This is the faith with which I return to the South. With this faith we will be able to transform the jangling discords of our nation into a beautiful symphony of brotherhood. With this faith we will be able to work together, to pray together, to struggle together, to go to jail together, to stand up for freedom together, knowing that we will be free one day.

This will be the day when all of God's children will be able to sing with new meaning "My country 'tis of thee, sweet land of liberty, of thee I sing. Land where my fathers died, land of the pilgrim's pride, from every mountainside, let freedom ring."

And if America is to be a great nation this must become true. So let freedom ring from the prodigious hilltops of New Hampshire. Let freedom ring from the mighty mountains of New York. Let freedom ring from the heightening Alleghenies of Pennsylvania!

Let freedom ring from the snowcapped Rockies of Colorado!

Let freedom ring from the curvaceous peaks of California!

But not only that; let freedom ring from Stone Mountain of Georgia!

Let freedom ring from every hill and molehill of Mississippi. From every mountainside, let freedom ring.

When we let freedom ring, when we let it ring from every village and every hamlet, from every state and every city, we will be able to speed up that day when all of God's children, black men and white men, Jews and Gentiles, Protestants and Catholics, will be able to join hands and sing in the words of that old Negro spiritual, "Free at last! Free at last! Thank God almighty, we are free at last!"

Martin Luther King, 28 August 1963

A freedom rally to celebrate the release of Nelson Mandela, who shared Martin Luther King's dreams.

This poem and the song opposite, and the speech on p.82, all express a similar theme – the longing for freedom.

Caged Bird

[1] A free bird leaps
on the back of the wind
and floats downstream
till the current ends
and dips his wing
in the orange sun rays
and dares to claim the sky.

[2] But a bird that stalks
down his narrow cage
can seldom see through
his bars of rage
his wings are clipped and
his feet are tied
so he opens his throat to sing.

[3] The caged bird sings
with a fearful trill
of things unknown
but longed for still
and his tune is heard
on the distant hill
for the caged bird
sings of freedom.

[4] The free bird thinks of another breeze
and the trade winds soft through the sighing trees
and the fat worms waiting on a dawn-bright lawn
and he names the sky his own.

[5] But a caged bird stands on the grave of dreams
his shadow shouts on a nightmare scream
his wings are clipped and his feet are tied
so he opens his throat to sing.

[6] The caged bird sings
with a fearful trill
of things unknown
but longed for still
and his tune is heard
on the distant hill
for the caged bird
sings of freedom.

Maya Angelou

Mountains o' Things

The life I've always wanted
I guess I'll never have
I'll be working for somebody else
Until I'm in my grave
I'll be dreaming of a life of ease
And mountains
Oh mountains o' things

To have a big, expensive car
Drag my furs on the ground
And have a maid that I can tell
To bring me anything
Everyone will look at me with envy and with greed
I'll revel in their attention
And mountains
Oh mountains o' things

Sweet lazy life
Champagne and caviar
I hope you'll come and find me
Cause you know who we are
Those who deserve the best in life
And know what money's worth
And those whose sole misfortune
Was having mountains o' nothing at birth

Oh they tell me
There's still time to save my soul
They tell me
Renounce all
Renounce all those material things you gained by
Exploiting other human beings

Consume more than you need
This is the dream
Make you pauper
Or make you queen
I won't die lonely
I have it all prearranged
A grave that's deep and wide enough
For me and all my mountains o' things

Mostly I feel lonely
Good good people are
Good people are only
My stepping stones
It's gonna take all my mountains o' things
To surround me
Keep all my enemies away
Keep my sadness and loneliness at bay

I'll be dreaming, dreaming, dreaming.../
Dreaming....

Tracy Chapman

Your view of the world

Do you have views you feel strongly about? Do things happen in the world which anger you and which you believe should be changed?

Write out a list of your feelings about the world you live in, perhaps in the form of a poem or song. You might use an approach like this one:

> *'I live in a world I do not like...*
> *I get fed up with the way...*
> *I am angered by...*
> *I am upset by...*
>
> *But if I must live in this world,*
> *I will protest against...*
> *I will fight for...*
> *I will change the way...'*

Alternatively, contrast your dreams against reality, using the first two lines of Tracy Chapman's song to start you off:

> *The life I've always wanted*
> *I guess I'll never have*

"I Have a Dream"

Reading aloud

Ask a good reader to read this speech aloud (see p.82). Then in small groups, try a reading of this speech (or part of it) with the aim of rousing the feelings of the audience who will hear it. Experiment with the way you read it. For example:

- The whole group might read the first and last paragraphs in unison.
- Each person might take turns to read each paragraph.
- Alternate – the whole group reads every other paragraph.

Now tape-record your reading or perform it 'live' to the class.

Understanding

In groups, discuss and note down your answers to these questions:

GOOD	EVIL
American dream 'All men are equal'	Slave-owners Slaves

1. Throughout *"I Have a Dream"*, **good** is compared with **evil**.
   Make a chart like the one opposite, on which you note all the words associated with good, and all the words associated with evil:

   What do you notice about the words you have put down in each column?
   Try to match together any opposites.
   Discuss the meaning of any words or phrases you don't know.

2. It has been said that this speech has a musical quality, like a hymn. Pick out any features of the speech which remind you of a hymn.

3. What impact does this speech have on you? Looking closely at the language used in the speech, discuss and note down some of the ways in which it might have roused the feelings of a mass audience.

Optimist or pessimist?

What is your view of the future? Are you an **optimist** or a **pessimist**? Choose *one* subject about which you feel generally optimistic or pessimistic. The list may give you some ideas:

> the environment,
> race relations,
> wealth and poverty,
> nuclear weapons,
> space travel,
> work and leisure.

Taking the view of the future you are more inclined to support, draft the script for a speech you would like to make to people who have the power to change things – to the local council or to Parliament.

Begin your speech either   with, *"I have a dream..."*
                            or   with, *"I have a nightmare..."*

A freedom/cage poem

When you have read *Caged Bird* on p.84, and studied the Techniques section on pp.88-89, try writing a similar poem yourself. Use the idea of a creature trapped in a human world, who is longing for freedom. Here are some ideas you might choose from:

> fish   : fish tank/sea
> hen   : battery farm/
>   free range
> lion   : zoo/jungle
> horse : circus, police,
>   riding stable/
>   moors
> rabbit : laboratory/
>   fields

If you like, use the same form as *Caged Bird* to help you to organise what you have to say.

TECHNIQUES

Appreciating poetry

When you discuss poetry, you are looking at *how* the poet uses language to say something to the reader. A poem has no single right meaning – the meaning lies in the way you *respond* to it. However, you can guide yourself into a fuller appreciation of poetry by understanding more about the poet's *craft*. This section helps you to look at some of the ways poetry is crafted using *Caged Bird* and *Mountains o' Things* as examples.

1. Form

All poems and songs have a form – that is, an overall shape and structure. Much traditional poetry was written with a pre-set form, such as the sonnet or the ballad. If you were to write a sonnet, you would know in advance the number and length of lines as well as which rhyming scheme to use. Many modern poets and songwriters do not follow such conventions – they prefer the meaning to determine the form.

- Look closely at the form of both *Caged Bird* and *Mountains o' Things* and the way each looks on the page.
  How random or deliberate do you think the form is in each case?
  Does the form help to express the message of each writer?

2. Imagery

Imagery is a comparison of one thing with another. It is used in poetry, as in all writing, to stimulate your imagination and understanding of the thing being compared. In *Caged Bird*, the image of a caged bird is used to suggest imprisonment, and a flying bird to suggest freedom.

- Make a list of all the words used to suggest freedom and imprisonment, in this way:

FREEDOM	IMPRISONMENT
leaps	stalks
wind	cage

- What do you notice about the words used in the poem to suggest **freedom** and **imprisonment**?

- Make a similar list of the words used in *Mountains o' Things* to suggest **dreaming** and **reality**. What do you notice about these words?

3. Rhythm

Most poetry is intended to be read aloud – it is like a spoken form of music. As in music, rhythm is simply the pattern of beats or stresses upon words or word syllables. Much traditional poetry has a pre-set number and pattern of stresses in a line. But in modern poetry, the rhythm is usually freer and less calculated.

In *Caged Bird*, there is no set rhythm, but when you read it aloud, you will find that your voice naturally emphasises some words or syllables, but runs lightly over others. For example, in stanza 5:

> '... The frée bird thínks of anóther bréeze
> and the tráde winds sóft through the síghing trees ...'

Choose any stanza from the poem and practise reading it aloud.

- Note where the stresses fall, in the same way as the example.
- Can you see any pattern to the words you are emphasising?
- How do the stresses help the meaning of the stanza?

4. Rhyme

Rhyme is also a link between poetry and music – particularly song. Rhyme is where one word exactly echoes the sound of another, like *cage* and *rage*. Traditional poetry is well known for using a set rhyming pattern at the end of each line but modern poets use rhyme more flexibly. Here are some types of rhyme used in *Caged Bird*:

Assonance: this is where the vowel sound of a word echoes another in the same line or close to it, for example in stanza 1:
'... a fr*ee* bird l*ea*ps ...'
'... and d*i*ps his w*i*ng ...'

Alliteration: this is where the first letter of two or more words in a line are repeated, for example in stanza 5:
'... his *sh*adow *sh*outs on a nightmare scream ...'

Half-rhyme: this is when the final consonants of two words agree:
leap*s*/dip*s* (1); clippe*d*/tie*d* (2); law*n*/ ow*n* (4).

Now look at the use of rhyme in *Caged Bird*.

- Find any examples of rhyme, either end-of-line, or mid-line, which emphasise the bird's desire for freedom.
- Now find examples of rhyme which stress the bird's imprisonment.
- Using what you have learnt about rhythm and rhyme, try a reading of the first two stanzas bringing out the contrast between the life of the free bird and that of the caged bird.

8 · Instructing

Drawing shapes

Ask for a volunteer to lead this exercise. The rest of you will need a sheet of graph paper, a ruler and pencil. The person who has volunteered to be the *instructor* will use the diagram on p.92, but the rest of you should not look at this diagram until the exercise is completed.

The instructor's job is to tell the class how to draw a diagram which looks exactly like the one on p.92. For example s/he might begin by saying:

First I want you to draw a rectangle, with the two short sides running at the top and bottom of the rectangle. The top side starts two centimetres down from the top edge of the graph paper, and two centimetres in from the left-hand edge of your paper...

Try this exercise at least twice.
First occasion:
nobody is allowed to ask the instructor questions.
Second occasion:
the instructor may answer questions.

On which occasion was your drawing closer to the instructor's original? Why do you think this was?

How to make a paper water-lily

For this exercise, each of you will need a square piece of paper kitchen roll or a table napkin. Follow the instructions on p.93 for making a water-lily.

How successful is your table decoration?
Do you think the instructions were clear enough?
Do you think that they could be improved at all?

Can you instruct?

You will need to bring a game or some simple equipment to your English lesson for this exercise. Show a partner or a group how to perform one of these skills:

If you are the instructor, turn your back on the person to whom you are giving instructions. The results might be amusing!

- wiring a plug
- plaiting hair
- tying a knot/tie/bow
- assembling a bridle/ tying a fly for fishing
- casting wool on to knitting needles
- solving a puzzle – Dimaxion, Rubik's cube, metal puzzles, etc.
- using a word-processor

Drawing shapes
(See exercise on p.91)

Instructions for Making a Water-lily

1. Fold paper in half and half again.

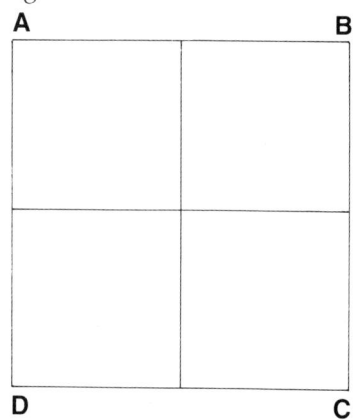

2. Take each corner in turn and fold to the middle.

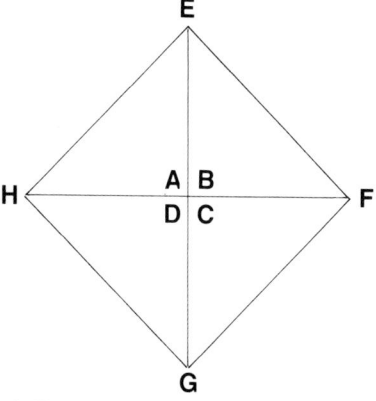

3. Take each new corner in turn and fold to the middle again.

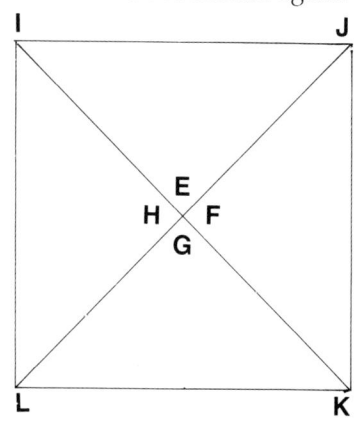

4. Turn the new square over and again fold each corner in turn to the middle.

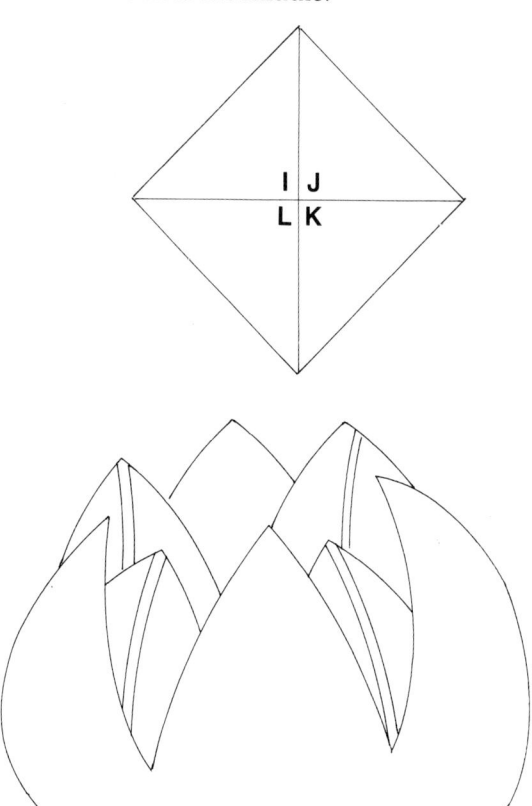

5. Hold the centre of the square between finger and thumb to keep the corners in place. Bring each single flap in turn from the back over the top to form a leaf. Bring over the four remaining flaps in turn to form outer leaves.

(from *How Do I Learn?* F.E.U., 1981.)

SURVIVING SHYNESS

The last of our psychological quizzes looks at being shy. Written especially for IS

Your heart begins to pound, you feel the blood rushing to your face and your tongue feels firmly attached to the roof of your mouth. No, you're not watching *A Nightmare On Elm Street*, you've become the victim of a sudden attack of shyness.

Of course, not everyone who suffers from shyness goes through these kinds of agony. Shyness, like any other bit of your personality, is a matter of degree. Chronic sufferers find every aspect of their lives affected by it. Not many of us fit into this category, but almost everyone suffers at some time or other.

In fact, the vital statistics of shyness are that four out of every five people are seriously affected by it at some time in their lives. Encouragingly, only half of that number will be suffering at any one time. This means that even if you're a shy person now, there's a good chance you won't always be.

What is shyness?

But what exactly is shyness? As a feeling, it's simply being uncomfortable in other people's presence, usually because you're worried that they're going to reject you. And although shy people are sometimes told off for being arrogant, being shy also puts you at a distinct disadvantage in at least four other ways.

● Shy people find it much more difficult to make friends or meet new people.

● They also run the risk of being underestimated, because teachers and bosses tend to assume that silence implies ignorance.

● More generally, shyness makes it difficult to communicate effectively with other people, which can interfere with every aspect of your life.

● And then there's the sad fact that people affected by chronic shyness often become very lonely and depressed by their lack of confidence.

Mistaken identity

So what makes a person shy? There's no evidence that it's an hereditary condition, though some researchers are convinced that the tendency to become shy is passed on from generation to generation. It's much more likely that shyness is a response you learn as you're growing up. Perhaps you've watched someone in your family suffer — and are modelling yourself on them. Or it could be that you've never had the chance to acquire the right social skills to deal with particular situations — if you grow up on a farm on the Isle of Arran, for instance, you're unlikely to be a dab hand at speaking to a room full of strangers.

It may even be a case of mistaken identity. If you were a quiet, thoughtful child, there is a fair chance that you grew up with "Oh, you're just shy" ringing in your

UNDER ANALYSIS

...ES by Dr John Nicholson

ears. This kind of comment often becomes a self-fulfilling prophecy. If you're told that you are shy often enough, you not only come to believe it, but to act it too.

Situations and stages

Of course, there are some situations when we're all prone to attacks of shyness. Starting a new school, beginning a new job, meeting your boyfriend/girlfriend's parents for the first time — these are all situations in which even the most confident among us tend to feel at least a little nervous.

There are also certain stages in life when you're more likely to suffer from shyness — for example, when you are a teenager. As far as teenage "ailments" are concerned, shyness is a front runner! It's no coincidence that this is also a time when you are moving away from the simple world of childhood certainties, based on parents' and teachers' views of the world, and trying to tackle the first challenge of adulthood — deciding for yourself exactly who you are. Indeed, becoming aware of your identity, and learning to accept the "new you", is often a major step on the road towards overcoming shyness.

Self-analysis

Try this quick bit of self-analysis to find out just how much you suffer from shyness. Think about each statement carefully, and answer True or False according to how accurately it describes the way you feel and usually act.

	True	False
1. I rarely worry about making a good impression	☐	☐
2. Generally, I feel very conscious of myself and the way I am behaving	☐	☐
3. I often worry that I put people's backs up by going about things in the wrong way	☐	☐
4. My daydreams don't often involve me	☐	☐
5. I find it difficult to walk past a mirror without checking my appearance	☐	☐
6. I don't often stop to think about why I said something	☐	☐
7. I don't really care what other people think of me	☐	☐
8. I sometimes have the feeling that I'm floating in the air, watching myself	☐	☐
9. The good thing about being shy is that it gives you a chance to stand back, observe others and then act more intelligently	☐	☐
10. When I start talking to someone, I always seem to find something to say	☐	☐

SCORING

For questions 2, 3, 5, 8 and 9 score 2 points for each TRUE answer and zero for every FALSE. For questions 1, 4, 6, 7 and 10 score 2 points for each FALSE and zero for each TRUE. The higher your score, the more shy you are. A score of 12 or more suggests you are ill-at-ease in the presence of others, and self-conscious even when you are alone.

There are actually two different forms of shyness — "public" and "private". Look at your answers again. If you answered FALSE to questions 1, 6 and 10 and TRUE to questions 3 and 5, then you suffer from public shyness. This means that you worry about behaving badly. If you answered TRUE to questions 2, 4, 8 and 9, you are suffering from private shyness. Private shyness is all about feeling bad — on the inside.

Most shy people suffer to some extent from both types of shyness. Public shyness is the most damaging type, since it affects the way you behave and perform in front of other people, and stops you doing yourself justice. Publicly shy people rarely become leaders, because no-one notices them.

Privately shy people, on the other hand, know how to present themselves, but they pay a price. They learn to hide their anxiety behind a "confident" and competent mask, but can end up feeling sad, isolated and misunderstood.

If your overall score was less than 6, you are rather confident and outgoing, and rarely find other people intimidating. Be careful, though, not to let your confidence lead you into making snap judgements about people, and so miss out on opportunities to make new friends.

If you scored highly, it's a fair bet that you are unhappy with the way you are at the moment. Researchers have found that only one in five shy people are happy. And those of you who are regularly crippled with shyness attacks won't be comforted by the notion that it may be "just your age". So what can you do to beat the cowering wallflower syndrome?

Shyness Survival Kit

1. Remember that some situations, like job interviews and oral exams, are frightening to everyone. Don't think that shyness in these situations is due to some failing in you.

2. If you find it difficult to talk to people, stop trying to think of new things to say. Why not ask them questions? Most people really enjoy blowing their own trumpets, and everybody appreciates a good listener.

3. Try not to run away from everyday situations that make you nervous. They will just seem even more frightening next time. Whatever it is, take a deep breath, tell yourself that you can do it, and grab the bull by the horns!

4. If particular situations make you feel very nervous, for example returning a faulty jumper to a shop, take along a friend for moral support.

5. Make a list of all the positive characteristics you have. Get a friend to check it and maybe add some attributes you may have overlooked in your modesty. Keep the list somewhere handy and use it to boost your confidence in moments of doubt.

6. Set yourself targets: for example, resolve to say hello to four strangers next week. Start with people you see every day in the bus queue or nodding acquaintances at school or work. After all, practice makes perfect.

7. Finally, remember that shyness does have some advantages. It is often much better to be thought of as "quiet and unassuming" than as "pushy" and "aggressive".

Illustration/Mark Bannerman

COLLECTING ALUMINIUM DRINKS CANS IS AS EASY AS ONE, TWO, THREE.

Don't trash it... Cash it!

THE ALUMINIUM CAN RECYCLING ASSOCIATION

Collect used aluminium drinks cans

Take to Recovery Centre

Bale For Transport

Remelt

Rolled into coilstrip

Made into cans

Filled

Back to the consumer

Aluminium is the 100% recyclable metal container material.

So after you've helped collect the drinks cans, they go back to the aluminium rolling mill. Then they're re-melted, rolled into coil strip, made into new cans, filled. And then sold again.

And it takes 95% less energy to remelt used aluminium cans than to make aluminium from raw materials. And that's why every aluminium drinks can is worth money.

Saving cans not only helps save energy, but also helps save natural resources, and improves the environment by reducing household waste and litter too.

So to collect aluminium drinks cans to help the environment and put money into your fund raising effort.

Your local collection organiser is:

THE ALUMINIUM CAN RECYCLING ASSOCIATION
FOR MORE INFORMATION CONTACT:
THE ALUMINIUM CAN RECYCLING ASSOCIATION
I-MEX HOUSE, 52 BLUCHER ST, BIRMINGHAM B1 1QU
TEL: 021-633 4656   FAX: 021-633 4698

1 TEST them
(They're not magnetic)

The magnet test. This is very important because not all drinks cans are made from aluminium. Test the side — not the top — the inside of your fridge door. Aluminium is not magnetic so keep only those cans that the magnet does not stick to. Some cans have the (Al) or (Alu) symbol, those are aluminium too.

BAG them 2

To save space when you are collecting, and for easy storage, put the ring pull inside the can and then crush the can, before you put it in the bag.

3 CASH them

Plastic refuse bags are ideal for keeping your can collection in. When your bags are full, store your cans in a suitable place, it could be a garage, spare room or garden shed. Then check with your organiser what to do next. Your organiser may arrange to take away your collection for you, or ask you to take your collection to a special place.

The Aluminium Can Recycling Association is helping your fund raising effort to make money, by promoting recycling of used aluminium drinks cans.

That's why the aluminium industry will pay you through your local official recovery centre at least 30p for every kilo of aluminium drinks cans you collect. (That's about 50 cans).

At that rate, there's an estimated £20,000,000 worth of aluminium drinks cans thrown away each year. And that's a lot of money going to waste!

So don't just sit there, start collecting!

Collecting aluminium drinks cans is as easy as ONE, TWO, THREE. Here are some easy guidelines to remember when you and your friends are collecting.

Write a guide on one of the following topics. To help you plan your guide, read Techniques on pp.100-101.

Instruction booklet on a hobby

Write an instruction booklet which introduces beginners to a hobby or interest in which you are involved. Here are some examples of topics you might choose:

- How to choose and look after a pet.
- How to build a model, a canoe, a computer, a musical instrument.
- How to start and run a discotheque, a band.
- How to ski, ride, windsurf, skate.
- How to play snooker, squash, American football, badminton.
- How to choose and maintain a piece of equipment – a scrambling bike or racing cycle, a bridle and saddle, a boat, a fishing rod, tent.
- How to set up and run a club, a campaigning group, a charity, a business, a school bookshop or tuckshop.
- How to exercise, diet, use make-up, dress well – on a budget.
- How to compete – swimming, racing, dancing, and so on.

A safety guide to...

If there is a topic on which you have some expertise, consider writing a survival guide for people with less knowledge than you. Choose one of these topics:

1. *Safety in the home – a guide for the family*
   You might choose to focus on one subject such as: fighting a fire, safety for young children, security against break-ins, first aid in the home, safety for pets.

2. *Keeping safe in danger sports – a guide for beginners*
   e.g martial arts, skiing, sailing, riding.

3. *Safety for teenagers* – to include sections on babysitting, newspaper rounds, nights out, on a new date, in a crowd, while travelling.

A survival guide to...

Imagine you have been asked by a teenage magazine to write a 'survival guide' to a typical teenage concern, as part of a series entitled, *It Needn't Be A Problem...*

The magazine's editor has sent you a copy of the article by Dr John Nicholson on pp.94-95, as a model of what is required. The editor has asked you to choose a topic from this list:

Your guide should be presented as attractively as possible using magazine design elements such as an eye-catching title, headings, columns, and boxes for the questionnaire and 'survival kit'.

- Surviving embarrassment
- Making friends
- Going to a party/ concert/ discotheque
- Taking a Saturday/ evening job
- Surviving parents
- Going out on a first date
- Fashion on a shoestring
- Going on holiday

A guide to a 'greener' life

Imagine that you are a member of a real or fictitious environmental group which campaigns for a 'greener' way of living. Suppose that it has commissioned you to design and write a campaign leaflet (like the one on pp.96-97), to advise people of your own age how they might support one of these issues:

- Stop 'the Greenhouse Effect'
- Better recycling facilities
- Ban the motorcar
- Save the whale/elephant/ panda/dolphin etc.
- Ban smoking
- Conserve energy
- Use 'ozone-friendly' products
- Ban/develop nuclear power

You may need to find out more about your subject by using school resources, the library and writing to pressure groups like Greenpeace and Friends of the Earth.

TECHNIQUES

Giving instructions

When you give guidance on how to do something, whether it is writing an instruction booklet, or giving directions, you are an authority. You have a knowledge or an expertise which you can pass on to other people. Here are some of the ways to write a clear and readable guide:

1. Research
You may know your subject so well that you do not need to research. For example, if you are a judo black belt and teach judo to others, you are probably expert enough! But if you have any doubts about your subject, check what you do know, then find out more.

If you find a library book on your subject, do not be tempted to copy it. Your guide will be much more convincing if it is written in your own words and draws from your own experience.

- Where can you find out more? When you have chosen which guide you intend to write, make a list of all possible sources of information: at home, in school, where you live, and nationally.

2. Readership
Who will be reading your guide?
Take care to consider the needs of the people who will be reading it.

It may help you to look at guides other than those in this chapter – for example, the Green Cross Code for children, or a guide to opening a bank account for students. Discuss how appropriate you think the use of text, visuals, headings and lay-out are for the specified readership.

3. Organising

Make a plan in which you organise what you have to say under clear headings. An instruction booklet on how to start a hobby such as judo might comprise a series of paragraphs with these headings:

> 1. *Introduction – Why you enjoy judo*
> 2. *Cost*
> 3. *Equipment and clothing*
> 4. *Time needed*
> 5. *Safety regulations*
> 6. *Your first lesson*
> 7. *Conclusion – Practice makes perfect*

4. Presenting

Present your guide so that it is both attractive and readable. Depending on its purpose, you can do this by using:

– a front cover, illustrated and titled,
– a Contents page,
– clear handwriting, or typing/word-processing it,
– attractive headings and sub-headings to sections,
– points of instruction numbered and spaced so that they stand out,
– diagrams, drawings, photographs, tables and graphs.

5. Writing style

Your writing style should show clearly the relationship between you and your reader – you as the teacher, your reader as the learner. How does the style of each of these extracts indicate its relationship with the reader?

> *... Of course, there are some occasions when we are all prone to attacks of shyness. Starting a new school, ... these are all situations in which even the most confident among us tend to feel at least a little nervous ...*
>
> *If you find it difficult to talk to people, stop trying to think of new things to say. Why not ask them questions? Most people really enjoy blowing their own trumpets and everybody appreciates a good listener ...*
>
> *Aluminium is the 100% recyclable metal container material ... So after you've helped collect the drinks cans, they go back to the aluminium rolling mill. Then they're remelted, rolled into coil strip ...*
>
> *So don't just sit there, start collecting! Collecting aluminium drinks cans is as easy as ONE, TWO, THREE ...*
>
> *Don't trash it, cash it!*

9 · Complaining

STARTERS

Making a complaint

Have you ever made a complaint about something you have bought? In groups, describe an instance when you have had to make a complaint. How do you behave when you have to make a complaint?

Do you know what your rights are when you have bought something faulty? To check this, read *Complaining – as a consumer* on p.110. Have you ever been 'fobbed off'?
Has this article told you anything you did not already know?

The faulty shoes

You have bought a pair of shoes. A week later, there is a problem with them and you decide to take them back to the shop.
In pairs, take the roles of shop-assistant and customer. As shop assistant, decide whether you are going to make life difficult for the customer or not. Then act out the complaint.

Neighbour nuisance

Suppose that neighbours of yours are making a nuisance of themselves. Something has happened which makes you decide that you must act – now! Your family is out so you decide to confront the neighbour yourself. Choose one of these situations on the right:

In pairs, take turns to be the neighbour.
When you have finished, discuss how you felt in each role.

Bonfires
the smoke comes into your bedroom.

Noise
loud television/hi-fi/shouting/parties/DIY.

Rubbish
coke cans, cigarette and sweet packets are thrown into your garden or left in communal hallways.

Dogs
a vicious dog barks and snarls at you as you enter and leave your home.

How you complain

When you make a complaint, how do you behave? Are you:

– angry and aggressive?
– apologetic and embarrassed?
– polite but firm?

Choose to act out one of the two exercises again. This time, experiment with the way in which you complain. As the two neighbours, try out the complaint using different styles of behaviour. For example, both neighbours might be apologetic and embarrassed.

Which do you think is the best combination of behaviour? Which is the worst?

Case study : Holiday complaint

For this case study you will work in one group, which will be partnered with another group. One group will take the role of clients and work on the activities listed below. The partner group will take the role of the tour operator and follow the activities on the next page. Please read the documents on pp.106-109 for this case study.

Apollo Holidays is a well-established tour operator who specialises in package holidays by air to popular resorts of the Mediterranean. You have recently returned from an Apollo holiday at Torremolinos in Spain and feel you have grounds for complaint. You can choose whether you have entirely legitimate complaints, or whether you are the kind of customer who enjoys complaining. (See pp.**197-198** on Role play.)

1. First, as a group, decide who each of you will be. Make sure that the group chooses a range of characters from this list:

- a single man or woman, looking for an exciting social life,
- a person with a young family, living on a budget, who was looking for organised activities for the children,
- a retired husband/wife,
- a honeymoon husband/wife,
- a parent with two or three teenage children.

2. Taking the role of your chosen character, suppose there were various reasons why you did not complain to Apollo's representative at Torremolinos. Now that you are home, write a letter to the Customer Relations Department of Apollo Holidays setting out the full details of your complaint. (See pp.**199-200** for Formal letter writing.) These details might include:

- the travel arrangements to and from the hotel,
- hotel facilities,
- behaviour of the guests,
- a noisy environment around the hotel,
- the resort,
- excursions,
- the food,
- the weather,
- the surcharges,
- the attitude of the hotel management,
- the distance from the beach.

3. When you have received the reply to your complaint from Apollo Holidays, it is up to you whether you decide 'to take the matter further'. If so, you may arrange for an interview with members of Customer Relations to express your dissatisfaction with their reply. You may be prepared to accept a compromise or ask to be referred to ABTA (the Association of British Travel Agents) for arbitration.

The case study ends when the dispute between you has been resolved.

You work in the Customer Relations Department of Apollo Holidays. The company is committed to fair trading and great care is taken to see that clients are fully satisfied with their holiday, so that they will book again next year. All complaints are fully investigated by your department, to decide whether the company is liable to pay compensation. The main distinction to make is whether the complaint is about something which is within the company's control, or whether it is beyond the company's control. In the latter case, Apollo Holidays accepts no liability for compensation. Apollo prefers always to resolve disputes with clients itself, rather than refer cases to ABTA for arbitration, which might damage the company's reputation.

Before you receive your clients' letters of complaint:

1. As a group, study the Booking Conditions on p.108, carefully – section by section. Discuss the meaning of any technical language and check that you all understand what is being stated.

2. Also study carefully the Brochure Description on p.106. Compare this with section 3, of the Booking Conditions. Which hotel facilities might be unavailable to holiday-makers for reasons beyond Apollo's control?

3. Then consider the likely areas for complaints (see question 2 on p.104). Discuss which complaints against the company might be justified, and which unjustified, according to the Booking Conditions.

After you receive the letters of complaint:

4. In your group, consider each letter of complaint in turn, deciding which complaints are justified and which are not. Decide who deserves compensation and how much you might pay. Be guided by the chart giving the original cost of the holiday, as well as the compensation chart in Booking Conditions, section 1.

Then share out the work of writing a letter to each of your clients, to tell them of Apollo's decision in their case.

5. When your clients have received your letters, they may be dissatisfied with your reply. If so, arrange an interview with any dissatisfied client. The aim is to reach a compromise with them, so that they do not ask to be referred to ABTA.

The case study ends when the dispute between you has been resolved.

The materials for this case study – **Holiday complaint** – comprise a brochure description (below), booking conditions and a case history of a holiday complaint reported to the consumer magazine, *Which?*

COSTA DEL SOL
Torremolinos

ADVANTAGES

This resort is a non-stop party. In fact if you reach the two long sandy beaches early in the morning, you'll find them relatively quiet as everyone is still recovering from the night before! There are discos, nightclubs and everything in between – we defy you to get bored. There's good shopping in the centre of town and Malaga is within easy reach.

DISADVANTAGES

Lovers of traditional Spain will be horrified: what remains of the whitewashed houses and narrow lanes is now well inland. Nightlife is relentless and hectic…your parents would hate the place.

TRAVEL DETAILS

Transfer time from the airport: approx. 20 minutes.

HOTEL MARINA

Position: Set on the edge of the main road (traffic noise is rarely a problem though) and restaurant dotted fishing district of lively La Carihuela, the impressive Hotel Marina is just 400 yards from a sandy beach (chairs/umbrellas payable locally). Shops, bars and discos are all close by and bustling Torremolinos centre is about ¼ mile away.
Amenities: Large outdoor pool • Sun terraces (chairs/umbrellas payable locally) • Poolside bar • Well-kept garden • Main lounge • Card, TV and video lounge • Two bars • Restaurant – no smoking area • Four shops including jewellery and souvenir shops • Hotel accepts Access, Visa, American Express and Diners Club credit cards.
Meals: All meals are buffet service • Lunch and dinner have a daily change of menu and choice of main course.
Entertainment: Daily "Happy Hour" • Full evening programme • Nightly dancing in bar • Fancy dress shows • Flamenco nights.
Sports: Tennis court (local charge) • Table tennis • Sauna • Daily gym club • Volleyball • Windsurfing, water-skiing and sailing from beach • Golf (4 miles).
For children: Separate pool • Playground • Early meals (on request locally) • Full entertainment programme • Mini-club • High chairs • Cots.
Bedrooms: Telephone • All twins have bath, loo • Some have balcony • 3rd bed available • All singles have bath or shower, loo.
Our opinion: Enviably located in Torremolinos' lively Carihuela district this popular hotel is a fine choice for families and especially the young as there is no lift down to the restaurant on ground level.
Basis: HB • FB also available.
Official rating: 3-star.
Size: Rooms: 303. Floors: 7. Lifts: 3.

PRICES PER PERSON IN £'s INCLUSIVE OF AIRPORT TAXES & VAT

Accommodation		HOTEL MARINA			FLIGHT SUPPLEMENTS TO COSTA DEL SOL					
Holiday Number		SEAGP 1155								
Prices include		Twin B loo/ HB		Child Red	GATWICK	LUTON	BOURNEMOUTH	BIRMINGHAM	MANCHESTER	
No. of Nights		7	14							
Departures on or between	28 Apr-11 May	199	280	70%	£0	£0	£0	£0	£0	
	12-21 May	219	300	70%	£0	£0	£0	£0	£0	
	22-28 May	229	319	35%	£0	£0	£0	£0	£0	
	29 May-15 Jun	217	312	70%	£0	£0	£0	£0	£0	
	16-22 Jun	224	319	50%	£0	£0	£0	£0	£0	
	23-29 Jun	229	330	50%	£0	£0	£0	£0	£0	
	30 Jun-13 Jul	236	359	50%	£0	£0	£0	£0	£0	
	14-20 Jul	254	384	35%	£0	£0	£0	£0	£0	
	21 Jul-20 Aug	269	389	35%	£0	£0	£0	£0	£0	
	21-27 Aug	274	374	35%	£0	£0	£0	£0	£0	
	28 Aug-10 Sep	264	364	50%	£0	£0	£0	£0	£0	
	11-24 Sep	255	344	50%	£0	£0	£0	£0	£0	
	25 Sep-1 Oct	239	332	70%	£0	£0	£0	£0	£0	
	2-19 Oct	223	300	70%	£0	£0	£0	£0	£0	
	20-26 Oct	229	–	50%	£0	£0	£0	£0	£0	
Supplements per person per night	Rooms	SGL B or sh loo £5.75			All prices based on Gatwick Wednesday (day)/Sunday (night) flights. For all Sunday (day) flights add £14. Full flight details on pages 282/284.					
	Meals	FB £2.50								

3rd person reduction: 15% on all dates except 10% on deps 22-28 May and 21 Jul-27 Aug.

Remember to add insurance: up to 8 nts £13.00. 9 to 17 nts £17.00. For child reductions see page 7 of this brochure. Please read pages 290/1 for information and pages 288/9 for booking conditions.

BOOKING CONDITIONS

Your contract is with Apollo Holidays Limited. Apollo is committed to a policy of fair trading and great care is taken to ensure that you have a successful holiday. All of the arrangements for your holiday are governed by the following booking conditions and by the general information shown elsewhere in this brochure. These set out your commitment to Apollo and ours to you. In addition, your holiday involves the provision of various services by independent organisations and the conditions of their agreements with you are also referred to below. Apollo follows the recommendations of the ABTA Code of Conduct which is prepared in conjunction with the Office of Fair Trading.

1 Alterations By Us

In order to keep prices as low as possible, inclusive tour holidays are based on efficient use of aircraft and hotels and these arrangements are planned many months in advance.

To maintain this efficiency it may be necessary, on occasion, to make some alteration to your flight or holiday arrangements or even to withdraw a particular flight from our holiday range.

We will always tell you via your travel agent of any **SIGNIFICANT** change as soon as reasonably practical as long as there is time before your departure.

Occasionally the change may be **MAJOR**. Again, we guarantee to tell you via your travel agent as soon as reasonably practical.

A **MAJOR** change is defined as:

(i) An alteration to your scheduled time of departure or return landing of ten hours or more **or** a reduction of time in resort of ten hours or more

(ii) A change of U.K. airport.

(iii) A change of accommodation to a lower rating or, where the new accommodation is not featured in the brochure, to a lower official rating.

(iv) A significant change of resort.

If we advise you of a **MAJOR** change or if we have to cancel your holiday you can either:

a) accept any alternative offered:

b) rebook any other available holiday from us at brochure cost;

c) cancel your booking and receive a full and prompt refund.

Whichever choice you make we will compensate you on the scale below by a credit voucher against the brochure price of the revised arrangement of your choice **or** if you decide to cancel, in cash.

Date of notification to your Travel Agent

More than 56 days before departure	Nil*
56 – 29 days before departure	£20*
28 – 15 days before departure	£40*
Less than 14 days before departure	£50*

*Amount in £ per fare paying passenger

Important Note
The compensation payments referred to above do not apply in cases of cancellations or major change where these are caused by circumstances beyond our control, including those set out in clauses 3 and 6 below.

We reserve the right to change our published prices and you would be informed of any change via your travel agent at the time of booking.

2 Price Guarantee

Once you have booked your holiday we guarantee that the price will not be subject to any surcharge. The only circumstances in which you would be liable to pay any more than the price at which you have booked your holiday would be as a result of action by the UK or any foreign government such as a change in the rate or treatment of V.A.T. in relation to package holidays or the imposition of any new taxes or duties which we were required to charge and/or collect on behalf of such government.

3 Brochure Descriptions

All brochure descriptions are advertised by us in good faith and every care is taken to ensure their accuracy. However, since we include so much detail and since the brochure is prepared up to 12 months in advance, there may be occasions when an advertised facility or entertainment is not available during your own particular holiday. Certain facilities (e.g. swimming pools, watersports, lifts, air-conditioning, etc.) require maintenance and sometimes have to be temporarily withdrawn from use for such work to be done. Outdoor activities, beach services and watersports for example may not operate for reasons such as unstable weather conditions or lack of support, or golf courses, bowling greens, etc. may be closed for maintenance or private competitions. Similarly, there may be occasions, especially during the low season, when certain advertised schedules, entertainments or amenities are changed, cancelled or curtailed. Further, the operation of certain amenities and facilities may be subject to local licensing laws or religious holidays. Government or local authority restrictions may also dictate that an hotel or apartment limits certain facilities e.g. air-conditioning or water supply, in the cause of conservation.

4 Conditions Of Carriage

When you travel with a carrier, for example on an aircraft, ship or coach, the Conditions of Carriage relating to that airline, shipping company or coach operator will apply to you. These conditions, some of which exclude or limit liability in certain circumstances and are often the subject of international convention between countries, can be inspected at your travel agents. Furthermore, other independent organisations involved in providing services included in your overall holiday arrangements may in some cases operate according to their own terms and conditions. In these cases those terms and conditions will apply to you.

5 Injury, Loss & Damage

Many services included in your overall holiday arrangements such as, for example, the services provided by the airline, hotel companies, coach or other transport operators and excursions booked through your Apollo representative in resort, are performed by independent organisations over whom Apollo have no direct control. Whilst we do not deny liability which may arise as a result of any acts or defaults of employees of Apollo, we do not accept any liability whatsoever arising from any acts or defaults of such independent organisations, their employees, agents or sub-contractors over whom we have no direct control but who may be involved in providing services included in your overall holiday arrangements. We do, however, take all reasonable steps to ensure that such organisations maintain high standards and conform with the laws and regulations of the country in which they are operating and we shall, of course, be willing to give reasonable assistance in helping to resolve any dispute which may arise between you and any such organisation but this should be registered and pursued with them at the time. Our Apollo insurance provides cover in respect of some of these aspects.

6 Travel Delays And Industrial Disputes

We are unable to accept responsibility for any aspect of your holiday and travel arrangements affected by matters over which we have no control including war or threat of war, riots and civil strife, terrorist activity, natural disaster, weather conditions, fire, flood, drought, an hotel's or apartment's late opening or early closing, breach of contract by an hotel or accommodation owner, temporary technical, mechanical or electrical breakdowns within an hotel or apartment, industrial disputes, governmental action, aircraft flow restrictions, airport regulations or technical problems to transport which may affect the service of hotels or apartments abroad or the scheduling of aircraft or other transport. However, Apollo Insurance offers cover in respect of some of these eventualities.

7 Misbehaviour

If you are prevented from travelling on an aircraft, coach, boat or other transport or from staying at your accommodation because, in the opinion of any person in authority (including, for example, police, pilot, cabin crew, security personnel, our representative or accommodation management), you appear by reason of alcohol, misuse of drugs or otherwise either to be unfit for travel or likely to cause discomfort or disturbance to other guests, we reserve the right to refuse you transport and/or accommodation and shall not be responsible to you for any loss or damage thereby incurred. Full cancellation charges will apply and no refunds will be given.

8 Solving Your Problems

Should you have any problem with any aspect of your holiday, you should notify our local representative immediately, so that he/she can try to resolve the problem.

Should our representative be unable to resolve your complaint and you wish to take up the matter after your return, you must write to the Customer Relations Department at our Head Office within 30 days of your return, setting out full details of your complaint. A full investigation will then be made. We cannot accept any complaints received after this time.

Disputes arising out of, or in connection with, this contract which cannot be amicably settled, may be referred to arbitration under a special scheme which, though devised by arrangement with ABTA, is administered quite independently by the Chartered Institute of Arbitrators.

Apollo will supply details of the scheme upon request which provides a simple and inexpensive method of arbitration on documents along with restricted liability in respect of costs. The scheme does not apply to claims for an amount greater than £1,500 per person, or £7,500 per booking. Neither does it apply to claims which are solely or mainly in respect of physical injury or illness or the consequences of such injury or illness.

AT YOUR SERVICE

Which? Personal Service gives advice and help to individual members when something goes wrong, and they find themselves unable to get redress following a complaint about faulty goods, poor service, shoddy workmanship or suchlike. More than 30,000 people subscribe to Which? Personal Service, and our Personal Service lawyers deal with over 3,000 cases a year. Here is one...

Holiday upset

Disaster struck the Carters' Spanish holiday before they had even left this country. Not only was the coach an hour late picking them up, but the driver got lost and headed north instead of south to Dover. As if that wasn't bad enough, the coach then broke down, so it was four hours before they finally got under way.

Things didn't get better when they reached Spain. The coach headed for the wrong resort, and by the time it got to the right one they were seven hours late. Mr Carter himself had to direct the driver to the apartments. Throughout this nightmare of a journey, there was none of the promised food and drink, since supplies had been put on the wrong coach.

Needless to say, by this time the Carters were looking forward to relaxing in their apartment. But their troubles were only just beginning.

The apartment was filthy and, despite promises by the reps, wasn't cleaned up. Mrs Carter spent a whole day scrubbing the place clean... The curtains in the living room couldn't be drawn, so anyone could look in.

The poolside bar promised in the brochure didn't exist, so the Carters couldn't even have a drink to help them unwind. And their three-year-old son didn't fare much better. There was neither the paddling pool nor the kiddies' club which had been described in the brochure.

The brochure had also said 'if it's peace, quiet and relaxation you're after, this is where you'll find it'. But the reps played loud music all day, so the Carters had to get away from the site to find any peace. They complained to the reps throughout the holiday, and also filled in a complaint form. They told us 'we were glad when the holiday was over'.

Mr Carter wrote to *Which? Personal Service*, and we prepared a letter for him to send to the holiday company claiming £300 compensation. When they didn't reply, we prepared further letters renewing the claim and threatening to sue. Finally we helped Mr Carter to issue a summons.

The company denied Mr Carter's claim. However, they did make an offer of £125 – but Mr Carter was determined to hold out for more. After attending a preliminary hearing of the case, the company sent Mr Carter a cheque for the £300 claimed plus £30 to cover the cost of issuing the summons.

Point of law
It's an express term of your contract with the tour operator that the holiday they provide will be as described in their brochure. And it's an implied term that the accommodation and transport will be reasonable. If they don't fulfil these terms, they are in breach of contract and you can claim compensation.

TECHNIQUES

Complaining – as a consumer

There's nothing more annoying than buying something that's not up to scratch, or having work done for you which just isn't right. But what can you actually do about it? Most of us seem rather timid about complaining but it doesn't have to end up in a bitter argument if it's handled properly.

If goods you have bought don't work, don't do what they're supposed to do, or don't match up to their description, colour or size, for example, then you are entitled to a refund provided you act quickly (you don't have to accept an exchange or credit note—remember you are *entitled* to your money back). If too much time has passed, you may still be able to claim compensation—usually the cost of a repair—and whichever you choose you're entitled to compensation if the goods caused you any additional loss —say if a faulty cleaning fluid damaged your carpet.

The same kind of rules apply when you buy services like dry cleaning or car repairs. Then, the work must be done to a reasonable standard and at a reasonable price—for example compared with what others might charge in the same area, unless you've agreed to a higher price to begin with—and in the time agreed (or in a reasonable time, if none was agreed).

TEN TIPS ON HOW TO COMPLAIN

☑ **Ask yourself what you want to achieve**
Complaining involves a lot of hassle—worthwhile if you get your money back. But with some complaints, you can expect no more than an apology (and perhaps a better deal for the next customer).

☑ **Know your rights**
But don't be too quick to quote them—the light touch might get a better result.

☑ **Complain as soon as possible**
Getting your rights requires prompt action.

☑ **Complain to the right person**
Don't vent your anger on the cashier or the telephonist, ask to see the manager (or whoever is in charge). Keep a note of their name and address, and *always* write to or telephone them personally.

☑ **Complain in person**
A personal visit often succeeds where a letter or phone call doesn't. But try not to lose your temper.

☑ **Follow up in writing**
Type or write legibly setting out (example below): the facts of the purchase—what you bought, when, and what you paid; the nature of your complaint; the legal position as you see it; what you wish done about it (for example a refund, immediate action and so on). Enclose copies of relevant documents such as bills or sales literature. Sending the letter by recorded delivery gives you proof of receipt.

☑ **Keep the paperwork**
Keep copies of all letters, notes of telephone calls and visits, and anything else which might help.

☑ **Stick at it**
Don't lose patience, some complaints can take a year or more to sort out. On the other hand, be ready to call it a day if you get a reasonable offer and know when to cut your losses.

☑ **Don't be afraid to seek help**
You can get help from a Citizens Advice Bureau or Consumer Advice Centre, Trading Standards Departments, trade association or ombudsman scheme. If you don't qualify for legal aid, some solicitors will give you an interview for as little as £5. The Which? Personal Service offers advice to its subscribers (write to Dept BJJ, 2 Marylebone Road, London NW1 4DX enclosing an sae).

☑ **Give praise where it's due**
Saying thank you not only helps keep good services good—it also builds up goodwill.

5 FOB-OFFS YOU SHOULD IGNORE

■ **"It's not covered by the guarantee"** 
Guarantees are offered as an addition to your rights—they give you the extra choice of using the guarantee to settle your complaint. Having a guarantee doesn't remove your legal rights against the seller. And you might do better with your basic legal rights if the guarantee doesn't cover your complaint—or if you're expected to pay for the labour or parts.

■ **"You didn't complain within 30 days (or three months/six months)"** 
Your legal rights last for six years—so don't let people tell you otherwise. If you want all your money back, reject faulty goods very quickly. But even if it's too late for this, you should still be entitled to a repair or compensation.

■ **"It's not our policy to give refunds"** 
If you buy goods which aren't of merchantable quality, fit for their purpose or what you were told they were, you're entitled to a refund if you act quickly. This applies even to goods in the sales, unless a defect was pointed out to you when you bought them (or the defect was so obvious that you should have noticed it). Displaying a notice which says, "No refunds given" is off-putting and against the law.

■ **"You'll have to take it up with the manufacturer"** 
If you've bought something faulty, it's up to the person who sold it to you to deal with it—not the manufacturer. But all too often, the seller will try to pass you on to the manufacturer. Don't accept this—tell the seller that it is his legal responsibility.

■ **"The fault was yours—it was the way you used it"** 
If the school shoes you bought your child fall apart after a few days' wear, don't be told they "weren't made to play in". School shoes are meant to be played in unless you're told otherwise when you buy them (for example, if the shop assistant says they're only fashion shoes). If you can't agree with a trader whether goods were faulty, ask if he belongs to a trade association. This may offer a free conciliation service.

Adapted from Which?

Complaining – as a communicator

If you want to complain by letter, *Which?* magazine suggests that you should use an approach like this:

> Your full postal address

> The date

> The name of the person or company you are writing to, plus the address.

```
Dear Sir/Madam, (manager's name if known)

On 9 November 1988, I bought a Kabashi video cassette recorder
K43 model from your shop (copy of receipt attached).

From the beginning, I had difficulty in ejecting cassettes.
Ten days after the purchase, a cassette jammed solidly, and
the unit no longer operates.

Under the Sale of Goods Act 1979, goods sold should be of
merchantable quality. The premature failure of the video
recorder shows there was an inherent fault at the time of
purchase, and it was not of merchantable quality.

Relying of the Sale of Goods Act, I therefore reject the goods
and expect to receive the full purchase price of £429.50.
Please also arrange to collect the recorder at your convenience,
and within 14 days of the date on this letter.

I look forward to hearing from you.

Yours faithfully, (sincerely)
```

> If your signature is difficult to read, print your initials and name after it.

If you want to complain in person, follow this advice:

- Think through what you intend to say in advance. But don't have a prepared script – this will sound artificial.
- Be firm and polite – never use insults. If you lose your temper, or sound angry and aggressive, you will only cause offence.
- Make eye contact with the person to whom you are making the complaint. S/he will listen to you more carefully, and perhaps take your complaint more seriously.
- If you are fobbed off with one of the excuses on p.110, keep to your original intentions. Simply repeat the message you wish to convey:

> *I'd like my money back.*
> *I'm entitled to my money back.*
> *Please give me my money back.*

> Imagine that you have decided to return the Kabashi video cassette recorder in person, to the shop where you bought it. In pairs take turns to play the role of the seller, and the client who is making the complaint. The 'seller' should alternate between using *real* grounds of rejection and one of the five 'fob offs' on p.110. Do you have any further advice to add to the list?

10 · Reporting

Probe into three bank accounts of MPs' girl

Lunch lockouts 'will hit pupils'

Scandal angers village in priest death riddle

Heroes save fire bomb family

Fury over Tory living in the sun

School mob kick out

Chase Pc fights for life after crash

STARTERS

The press release

A press release is essentially a news story in outline. It may often advertise the cause of a business enterprise, charity, or community group. (See the example of a press release on p.**114**.)

A press release also forms the basis of report writing because it has to obey these five basic rules:

> **What** is happening, **Who** is doing it, **Where** it is happening, **When** it is happening, and **Why**?

1. In pairs, work out the story behind one of the headlines on the facing page. Use the 'Five W's' above to help you. Then write a brief news story of about 30-40 words.

2. Write a press release for an event you have attended recently, e.g.:
   – a sports match,
   – a competition,
   – a concert/play/show/exhibition,
   – a meeting,
   – a disco,
   – a fundraising event – fete, jumble sale, sponsored walk.

The news story

Raiders hunted

Police were yesterday searching for two raiders who broke into a branch of Barclays bank in Linton, near Cambridge, and threatened three bank staff who later escaped. Police broke into the bank after a siege but failed to find the raiders.

1. Turn this news summary into a full news story, for a popular national daily paper.
2. Find an article from a local or national newspaper, and reduce it to the same length as this news summary.

The news interview

Can you think of anything you have done in recent years, which was, or might have been, reported in your local newspaper? For example: winning a competition; taking part in a sponsored event; helping somebody; having an accident; doing something brave, or foolish?

Take turns to interview each other about your 'newsworthy' experience, then use this material to write a short report with a headline.

DIDCOT RAILWAY CENTRE NEWS

July 1989

STEAM UP FOR DIDCOT'S AUTUMN GALA

It's full steam ahead at the Didcot Railway Centre in Oxfordshire for the Autumn Steam Gala on Saturday 30 September and Sunday 1 October, when there will be at least six of the Great Western Railway steam locomotives in action each day around the engine shed and pulling the trains.

There are lots of things to see apart from the engine in steam including demonstrations of the working of an old-style signalbox, inspecting the restoration of locomotives and carriages and having a last look at the Jessop Collection of steam paintings by David Weston and Colin Garratt which has been on display during the summer.

Didcot Railway Centre is open from 11am to 5pm but for visitors who want to see the locomotives being prepared for the days' activities the gates open at 8am. The special Earlyriser tickets cost £7 for adults (£5 for children and OAPs) and include a full cooked breakfast served in the Refreshment Room. The number of Earlyriser tickets is limited so early application is advised; they can be ordered from Great Western Society, Didcot, Oxfordshire, OX11 7NJ enclosing remittance and stamped addressed envelope.

The entrance to Didcot Railway Centre is at Didcot Parkway British Rail station served by Inter-City and Network South-East. By road it is on the A4130 three miles from the A34.

Editors: for further information please contact Jeanette Howse on
Didcot (0235) 817200

Great Western Society Didcot Oxfordshire

The selection of news reports which follows, is taken from contemporary and past newspapers, and from a current television programme.

The show will go on — and vive la difference!

By BAZ BAMIGBOYE

THE director of the £3million musical Metropolis emerged from crisis talks last night and pledged to open on time.

Frenchman Jerome Savary admitted there had been 'problems and arguments' with the producers of the extravagant show, which is due to have its premiere on Wednesday.

But he said: 'I work in a way that is different from British directors. That could be because I am a Frenchman. Vive la difference.' Previews of Metropolis began last Saturday at London's Piccadilly Theatre, and at least four songs have been axed. In addition, the attitude of M.Savary — who is regarded in France as a genius — was causing some concern. The show's general manager, Joanne Benjamin, described him as a 'volatile character' who would apparently vent his feelings about the production during the interval.

After last night's meeting with producer Michael White and composer Joe Brooks, M.Savary said: 'The show needs some work and some cutting. It is a good show but needs to be better. I have some problems with the language but no problems with the show. I will work on it till opening night and I will not leave it.' He was referring to unfounded rumours that he was to be replaced, and that security guards had been hired to keep him from the theatre. Mr White said: 'There are always meetings and problems before every big musical opens. Andrew Lloyd Webber has meetings every day on his new show.'

Metropolis, starring Brian Blessed and American actress Judy Kuhn, boasts £1.5million worth of spectacular sets designed by Ralph Koltai and special effects created by the team who produce the Star Trek movies.

It is based on Fritz Lang's classic 1920s film about a futuristic society of workers who toil below ground while elitists enjoy life above. Metropolis has to compete with other mega-musicals including Lloyd Webber's Aspects of Love, which has taken £3.5million in advances, and Miss Saigon, which has taken £1million.

from the *Daily Mail*

HAMPSTEAD SHOOTING CASE.

Fresh light was thrown upon the shooting of John Bellis by Maud Amelia Eddington, at Hampstead last week, during the proceedings at the inquest on the deceased.

It will be remembered that three pistol shots were heard at an old shop occupied by Griffiths and Co., where the part-proprietor, John Bellis, was found on the floor unconscious and bleeding from two bullet wounds.

Also lying on the floor was the young woman Maud Eddington, twenty-two years old. She was not injured, but was in a very hysterical and excited condition. Near her lay a revolver.

At the inquest Mr. George Griffiths, uncle of the deceased, gave evidence pointing to the great probability of a struggle having taken place owing to the deceased having grasped the revolver to prevent the girl from killing herself. This view was supported by Police-constable Stone and Mrs. Broad, the matron at the police-station.

The phrase uttered by Eddington on recovering consciousness was also urged in confirmation of the theory—which was now rapidly gaining support—that the girl meant to shoot herself. The phrase was reported to be: "It is your fault; I intended to shoot myself." This was taken at first to be addressed to the policeman who arrested her, but it was pointed out that a more likely theory was that these first words after recovering consciousness were addressed by Eddington to her lover.

The jury, guided by the coroner, took this view of the case, and found that the death of John Bellis was accidental, owing to his having struggled with Maud Eddington to prevent her attempted suicide.

Hampstead Tragedy. Maud Amelia Eddington, the girl who shot her sweetheart.

[We reproduce on this page] a portrait of Miss Eddington sketched in court.

Illustrated Mail, 26 January 1901

THE WRECKING OF A NORTHAMPTON MUSIC HALL.

An unrehearsed and unexpected turn wound up in a sensational style the week's performances at the Northampton Empire Music Hall, on the night of the 5th inst.

It arose out of the mysteriously sudden flight of one of the lessees with the takings, leaving nothing but a few coppers in the box-offices wherewith to pay the performers. There was, of course, a great hubbub; the hall was stormed, and the interior of the building, which is the largest place of entertainment in Northampton, was practically wrecked. Windows, doors, and fittings were smashed, curtains ripped down, and scenery destroyed by the infuriated crowd.

The chief sufferers by the disappearance of the proprietor were a large number of touring music-hall artists who were stranded without means, and fifty of Northampton's poorest children, who had been engaged for a spectacular display. In their distress the victims turned to a fellow performer more fortunately situated, viz., Mr. F. Morrison, who is known as "The American Hercules."

Mr. Hercules, who, perhaps because he is so very strong and has a "kiddie" of his own, is very tender-hearted, turned to his fellow-artists. "Boys," he said, "I guess we are in a fix, but it's worse for the 'kiddies.'" A man came up with two pounds' worth of coppers in a bowl. This the strong man took, and began doling out the coppers to the children. Twelve pennies each he gave them, but the money ran short, and 10s. was wanted. This he took from his own pocket. He also paid the railway fares of three of the artists, and sent them on their way rejoicing. Moreover, he gave guarantees to all their landladies for payment.

The Empire Music Hall has had an extraordinary history. Within the past four years three of its managers have fled in the night, leaving hosts of angry creditors, and this is the second time within a few years that artists have been stranded in the town through the disappearance of a manager.

Mr. Fulton Morrison, the saviour of the Music Hall Company at Northampton.

This transcript is from the television news programme, *Eyewitness*, which aims to give a dynamic style to its investigative news reports.

'The Irish Triangle'

Reporter Fishermen call it 'The Irish Triangle'. It's an area in the Irish Sea that in recent years has become the stage for many unexplained and bizarre happenings. There are cases of boats being dragged backwards, huge waves appearing from nowhere on calm days and boats simply disappearing. None of these incidents has been properly explained. So I went to fishing communities on *both* sides of the Irish Sea to investigate.

Conditions were perfect when the 78 foot trawler the *Angowrie* set to sea. It was a calm winter morning, just off the coast of Ireland. Her skipper and owner, Tom Stephenson, had put the *Angowrie* on a course along the Irish Sea with her nets trawling a thousand feet behind. They were steaming peacefully at three knots when disaster struck. Suddenly, the *Angowrie* crashed to a halt. Something powerful had caught the nets and was dragging her backwards. Then a shackle broke and the *Angowrie* was free. But Tom had lost £16,000 worth of equipment.

Tom I would say it was the most frightening experience I'd ever had. And that would apply to everybody on the boat and any fisherman that's caught on the Irish Sea. I wouldn't think it would matter who you asked, that would... you wouldn't get any worse than that, no.

Reporter There are similar stories on the Welsh side of the Irish Sea. Wendy Webster lost her husband, David, after a tragic accident on a beautiful day, early last September.

Wendy His body was found some 75 days after the accident.

Reporter 75 days? It's two months. My God. Wh'... where was he, where was he found?

Wendy Ummm... round the headland.

Reporter This coast, this coast here? Beyond this further headland.

... David Webster was one of four men on the 28 foot *Inspire*. His friend, Sam Skinner, was the only one to survive.

... So what did you see, Sam?

Sam Er... I turned round in the cabin. I could see a 6 foot wave coming over the stern of the boat.

Reporter What happened then?

Sam   Well, it swamped the boat and within a couple of minutes, the boat was upside down and sinking.

Reporter   The loss of the *Inspire* is just one of the dozens of mysterious incidents that have got fishermen on both sides of the Irish Sea worried.
In the past six years, 32 men have drowned and 17 boats have disappeared in unexplained circumstances.
But what really puzzles the fishermen is where these incidents have been happening. Every one of has been in the triangle of water between the coasts of Ireland and Great Britain – normally a safe place to fish.
The Irish fishing boat the *Summer Morn* gives us *one* clue as to what could be happening. Two years ago she was dragged backwards through the triangle for three hours, completely out of control. But *this* royal navy helicopter, pictured at the scene during the *Summer Morn*'s ordeal, indicates a submarine had snared the boat's nets. And Tom Stephenson also believes a sub caught *his* net.

Tom   Well, there's nothing else would do it. There's nothing down there would catch you. Only a submarine could pull your boat round and take you away backwards.

Reporter   The day after the *Inspire* went down, Fishguard undertaker, Jackie Jenkins, saw a strange sight off the breakwater.

Jackie   I noticed, er, looking seaward, um, a funny sort of wake, a froth, and I got my glasses, my binoculars, from the car and had a look seaward and it was definitely a submarine.

Reporter   It was a submarine behind the wash?

Jackie   Behind the wash.

Reporter   More subs are using the Irish Sea than ever before. The reason is simple. In previous years they have left their secret base in the west coast of Scotland and headed out north of Ireland. But in the strategic cat-and-mouse game our Navy plays with the Russians, the safest place to avoid detection is the Irish Sea.

from *Eyewitness, ITV*

Young Britain is growing up in a most alarming way

by Greg Hadfield and Tim Rayment

Q What was the time when you went to bed last night?

Percentage

In bed By...	1st year (11+) Boys	Girls	3rd year (13+) Boys	Girls	5th year (15+) Boys	Girls
9.00pm	23.3	24.3	6.0	8.7	2.7	3.3
9.30pm	16.5	22.3	8.8	12.6	3.3	5.2
10.00pm	27.5	24.3	23.4	22.7	11.9	15.6
10.30pm	12.6	12.7	24.5	21.9	20.0	22.8
11.00pm	9.1	8.7	16.7	16.7	23.7	22.4
11.30pm	3.9	4.0	8.9	8.6	17.5	15.2
12.00 midnight	3.6	1.9	6.0	4.5	9.8	9.0
1.00am	2.7	1.2	4.3	3.1	8.5	5.8
2.00am	.5	.3	.8	.8	2.2	.5
After 2.00am	.4	.2	.6	.3	.6	.2

Q Which adult do you get on best with?

Percentage

	1st year (11+) Boys	Girls	3rd year (13+) Boys	Girls	5th year (15+) Boys	Girls
Mother	28.3	32.3	28.0	38.8	29.0	37.4
Father	13.1	9.5	15.5	8.5	14.0	9.2
Both parents	43.4	40.8	36.9	26.2	28.8	21.7
Brother or sister	4.2	4.2	6.4	8.3	9.1	10.6
Relation	4.4	4.0	4.1	5.8	5.9	4.6
Teacher	.5	.3	.3	.6	.8	1.1
Friend	4.7	7.0	6.9	10.6	10.1	13.5
No one	1.4	1.7	1.5	1.1	.8	1.1

Q For how long did you watch television programmes (live or recorded) after school yesterday?

Percentage

	1st year (11+) Boys	Girls	3rd year (13+) Boys	Girls	5th year (15+) Boys	Girls
None	5.3	6.6	4.9	6.0	6.9	8.1
Less than 1hr	13.6	16.9	12.7	16.5	14.4	19.2
1-2hr	20.4	23.4	18.8	21.7	20.8	22.7
2-3hr	19.4	18.4	21.7	18.4	21.0	20.0
3-4hr	14.6	15.0	18.1	16.7	16.1	14.9
4-5hr	11.3	9.3	9.7	9.8	10.3	7.5
5hrs or longer	15.4	10.4	14.1	10.8	10.3	7.6

WHEN we are 11, we go to bed before News at Ten and get on well with our parents. At 12, one in three of us knows the taste of cigarettes. By 13, British teenagers are more likely to buy alcohol and tobacco than spend their money on books. At all ages, the nation's secondary pupils spend about as much time watching television as they do in the classroom.

These are among the findings of the biggest survey yet conducted into the lives of young Britons, to be published later this week. The result, a portrait of everything from loneliness to toothache, will become one of the most important social documents of our time.

The work has been undertaken by Exeter University's health education unit, from data supplied by more than 18,000 pupils aged 11 to 16. The pupils, at 121 schools throughout Britain, were asked 79 questions on confidential forms that have been developed over 10 years to encourage honest answers.

One government minister, told by The Sunday Times of the result, is so concerned that he has asked the researchers to see him tomorrow. "A lot of parents are going to be surprised," said John Butcher, under secretary of state for education. "Most will argue that these are someone else's children."

So what are they like, the young people in our homes and schools? Can they talk to their parents? What do they spend their money on? Is it true they don't do homework? To find out, we studied the statistics and travelled to Wiltshire to meet pupils at a typical comprehensive school.

Children at The Commonweal school in Swindon had all been set homework before our visit; but, to the alarm of Butcher and his colleagues, the national survey shows that many schools set little. In the fifth year, 47% of boys and 41% of girls had had no homework the day before. Similarly, one in three boys in the second year and one in four girls had not had homework. "A chilling phenomenon," Butcher said.

If they are not doing homework, how do our young spend their evenings? This much was plain: watching television.

In the first year, 41% of boys and 35% of girls watch for more than three hours; 15% of boys and 10% of girls for more than five. At 14, the figures start to drop. But even in the fifth year, 37% of boys and 30% of girls are still switched on for more than three hours, and 10% of boys and 8% of girls for more than five.

* * *

Books cannot compete. Half the first-year boys in the national survey, and more than a third of the girls, had done no reading for pleasure at home the day before. As

Today's children spend as much time in front of the television as they do in class and are less likely to use pocket money to buy books

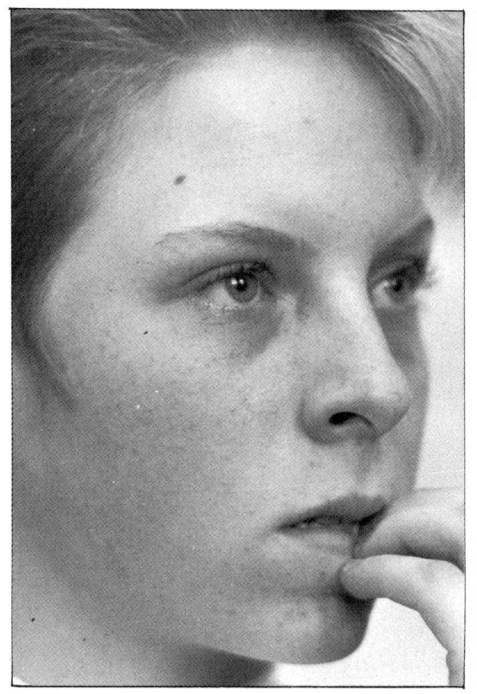

Melanie, with five babysitting jobs and weekends in a shop, earns £30 a week; Joe threw away his computer after the cat was sick on it

they got older, the number of book-readers fell. By the fifth year, 68% of boys and 56% of girls said they had not picked up a book the evening before.

"I never read," says Andy "Ozi" Oscroft, 16, a bright Commonweal pupil. "When I was little, I used to read horror books, but not now. I know reading improves you, but it's boring."

Those seeking evidence of greater equality will be depressed to learn that, at all ages, about 60% of girls help regularly at home, compared with 40% of boys.

Indeed, boys seem to enjoy a more active life. They spend more often on club subscriptions, bicycles, sports equipment, computer items, football matches, video hire and slot machines, while girls spend more often on pets, presents, and jewellery.

"Parents are a lot more scared about the safety of girls than of boys, which means girls are more likely to be kept in," says Elizabeth Hendry, a consultant psychologist and equality expert. "But the differences start on the day we are born, or even before, in the minds of parents."

In one respect, however, our four Swindon first-years were an exception. The two girls played computer games, the boys did not. But for Joe Aspinall, 11, there was a good excuse. "I did have a computer, but my cat was sick all over it," he explained. "I took it down the menders, but they couldn't fix it. All the chips were overheating." He threw it away.

* * *

By the fifth year, half the pupils were doing a regular job. Melanie Tuck, 15, who is taking six GCSEs, earns £30 a week. She works in a fruit shop at the weekend, and has five babysitting jobs.

An insight into family relationships is offered by the question, "Which adult do you get on best with?" In the first year, 43% of boys and 41% of girls answer "both parents", but as they get older the number falls, suggesting problems with one parent. By the fifth year, only 22% of girls still say "both" *(see table)*.

The survey follows a speech last week by Kenneth Baker, the education secretary, blaming the permissive 1960s for today's ills. But the Swindon parents — products of that decade — are tougher than Baker might imagine.

"My mum and dad don't like me having a boyfriend," said Samantha Hutchings, one of the fifth-year group. "They say it affects my schoolwork."

The first-years were set going-to-bed times such as 9 or 9.40pm, although some could get round it. "I can read from 9 to 10, but then I must put my light out," said Shane. "So I Sellotape my torch to the bedpost."

According to Malcolm Wicks, director of the Family Policy Studies Centre, we cannot easily measure whether the statistics are much worse for Shane's generation than for 10 or 20 years ago. "In Britain, we tend to take a rosy view of the past," he said. "However, the figures are alarming — not least on homework."

from The Sunday Times

ACTIVITIES

Styles of newspaper reporting

Group discussion
Working in a group, read the two articles from the *Illustrated Mail* on pp.116-117. Using the *Daily Mail* article as a comparison, discuss how you can tell that the article was written some time ago. Consider the use of:

> print; headlines; pictures; words; phrases and expressions; and period details e.g. 'Empire Music Hall'

Could the Northampton Music Hall story possibly have taken place today? Could the Metropolis story possibly have taken place in 1901?
Explain your answer fully in both cases.

Writing a news story
1. **Either,** write a modern version of the *Hampstead Shooting Case*, as if it were to appear in the pages of one of the national daily newspapers. If possible, get hold of a copy of your chosen newspaper and study its 'house style' – lay-out, writing style, use of headlines and pictures, and so on. Then write your report accordingly.
2. **Or,** write a continuation of the story of the Northampton Music Hall, as if it were to appear in a later issue of the *Illustrated Mail*. Use similar writing style as the original report. Choose one of these headlines or invent one of your own:

> MUSIC HALL THIEF IS CAUGHT!
> CHILD ACTOR IS FOUND BEGGING IN THE STREET
> HERCULES REVIVES THE MUSIC HALL

Television reporting

1. In groups, read the sound script, *'The Irish Triangle'*, for the television news programme, *Eyewitness* on pp.118-119. Remember that the aim of *Eyewitness* is to tell lively and dynamic news stories which should entertain as well as inform. As a group, see how far it is possible to change the impact of the script by the way it is read aloud. Work out two group readings of the script, making it:

   a) more dramatic and entertaining,
   b) more factual and informative.

2. Still in groups, discuss (and make notes on) what you think the viewers might see on the screen at any stage during this news report. How might the report make effective use of music and sound effects at given moments to enhance the suspense of the 'story'?

3. Work on your own to produce a complete film script for *'The Irish Triangle'*. (See p.**205** for advice.) Your script should give a very clear idea of what is seen on the television at each stage in the report, as well as giving directions for music and sound effects. Follow the advice given on how to write the voice-over and dialogue in 'shorthand'.

Radio reporting

In groups, make a news programme for radio. Imagine that the programme, called *Earwitness*, has a similar editorial policy to the one used in *Eyewitness* – that is, to investigate news items and to entertain the listener. Using a selection of national newspapers, find two news stories your group might 'investigate'. Then, drawing on the group's imagination, adapt the content of each news story for a radio script. Your programme editor has specified that all scripts should contain:

- basic information: what, who, where, when, why?
- reporter commentary,
- interviews with people involved,
- opposing points of view,
- an editorial overview,
- drama and suspense.

When you have worked out your programme script, allocate parts and make a tape-recording of your programme.

The medium and the matter

How much is the subject-matter of a news report influenced by the medium which presents it?

1. In pairs, read *Young Britain is growing up in a most alarming way* twice. Do you think that the article puts forward a neutral, or a particular point of view on the survey? Either way, how can you tell? Now discuss how the survey may have been reported if it had appeared in one of the media listed on the right:

   - a tabloid newspaper,
   - a popular teenage magazine,
   - an English teachers' journal,
   - a television news report.

2. On your own, choose *two* of these media, and for each one, write the first two or three paragraphs of the report/article/television script. Study examples of your two chosen media beforehand, to compare the differences in design, lay-out and reporting style.

TECHNIQUES

News reporting

You will need a range of national newspapers, preferably of the same date, for the group exercises in this section.

The purpose of most news reporting is to inform. However, some newspaper and television reports also aim to entertain.

> In groups, look at a selection of newspapers. Discuss which of these papers aim:
> – primarily to inform,
> – primarily to entertain,
> – to strike a balance between informing and entertaining.
>
> Compare the front page of the broadsheets (larger size), with the tabloids (smaller size). Is there any relation between a paper's size and its main aim?

Whatever the aim of a news report, it may use a wide range of language styles. These are:

1. Explaining

A report has to **record** and **explain** facts. When you are reporting, you have to decide:
– which facts are important,
– how to organise the information.

If you remember to follow the five basic rules of a press release, you will have the outline of a news story:

- WHO is involved?
- WHEN it is happening?
- WHERE it is happening?
- WHAT is happening?
- WHY?

The Five W's

2. Narrating

A news report which simply informs is not always interesting to read. The skill of certain reporters is in transforming a series of news 'facts' into an entertaining story.

- In groups, find several examples of news reports which tell a story from your selection of newspapers. Take turns to read these examples aloud, then discuss:

– which elements in each report remind you of a story?
– what are the common features of many 'news stories'?
– what is gained or lost by reporting a news event as if it were a story?

Like stories, all news reports are told from a particular viewpoint – that is, the way a reporter **sees** and **interprets** an event. This viewpoint may depend on factors such as the editorial policy of the newspaper or TV programme, the type of readership or audience, and the experience and opinions of the reporter.

- In groups, take each leading news 'story' in your selection of newspapers in turn. Read the first few paragraphs of the report, then discuss:

– what its viewpoint appears to be, and how you can tell what this is.
– which news report is the most/least obvious in its viewpoint, and why this might be.

3. Interviewing

News reports are not based solely on a reporter's experience of an event. They are also based on interviews with the people involved. The words of both 'expert' and 'ordinary' people are used to tell what happened, to give opinions and to express feelings. Their words may be quoted **directly**, or reported **indirectly**. (See p.**206** for Direct speech.)

> - Choose any news event, reported in your newspaper selection, which might be considered controversial. Ask one person to read this report aloud to the group then identify the various points of view expressed. What may be the purpose of providing more than one point of view? Is each point of view equally represented? If not, how does the report suggest a bias towards one particular view?

11 · Discussing

STARTERS

Would you survive in the desert?

Imagine that you have crash-landed in the Sahara Desert. The light, twin-engine plane containing the bodies of the pilot and the co-pilot, has completely burned. The rest of you are uninjured.

Before the engine caught fire, your group was able to salvage the items listed on the right. On your own, rank these items according to their importance to your survival, starting with '1', the most important, to '14', the least:

- flashlight
- jack-knife
- sectional air map of the area
- plastic raincoat
- magnetic compass
- compress kit with gauze
- ·45 calibre pistol
- bottle of 1000 salt tablets
- 1 litre of water per person
- parachute (red and white)
- a pair of sunglasses per person
- 2 litres of 180 proof vodka
- 1 top coat per person
- a cosmetic mirror

When everyone has finished the *individual* ranking, work in groups of about five. Now produce a rank order of the fourteen items as a *team*. When you have finished, compare both your individual ranking and the team ranking with the experts' ranking (given at the bottom of p.136).

Which ranking was closer to the experts' – your own, or the team's? Did group discussion help or hinder your accuracy?
Why might this have been?

A trip to Mars

Suppose you have been shortlisted with a group of others for a place on a space mission to set up a space station on Mars. Only two people will be chosen from the shortlist to go on this unique mission. On their return, the two will be offered lucrative contracts with publishers and film producers wishing to buy the 'rights' to their stories.

Each of you will be given a card which has written on it *one* of the following occupations:

- photographer
- biochemist
- medical student
- journalist
- computer programmer
- army officer
- school pupil
- artist/sculptor

In groups of five or more, take turns to argue your case for being chosen to go on the mission. Then discuss and agree on which two should be chosen to go, within a time limit of twenty minutes. Elect a spokesperson from your group to explain the group's choices to the class.

> This discussion on the *Wogan* show focused on the subject of whether violence on television affects the behaviour of young people. The guests invited to speak are known both for their expertise on the topic, and for their strongly held views.

> **Terry Wogan**
> programme host
> **Mary Whitehouse**
> of the National Viewers and Listeners Association
> **Ludovic Kennedy**
> television interviewer
> **Andrew Neil**
> editor of *The Sunday Times* and chief executive of Sky television.

How important is television really?

Wogan Do you take as serious a view as Mary does (or do you, Andrew,) of the influence that television has on young people?

Ludovic I don't think I know, and I don't think Mary knows what influence television has. My guess is that television doesn't have very much influence. If you have nothing but violence and nothing but sex, you may get people imitating violence and sex.

Mary And becoming desensitised. Violence is just a joke. There's nothing to shock you about violence.

Ludovic Ah yes, but you see, it depends whch way it comes. You think that television either causes or exacerbates violence in society. I think it's the other way round. I think...

Mary No, I don't, listen...

Ludovic I think, I think... just let me finish now I've started... I think that, I think that television reflects society both in violence and to a certain degree in sex, though I'd like to keep them separate...

Mary Yes but, yes but, you know what... sorry.

Wogan But what about you, Andrew? Do you feel it has the influence? I mean, for instance, Mary, you take exception, or you have taken considerable exception to *EastEnders* and you say that people, young people in particular, will be influenced in their behaviour from watching it. But equally, there are a number of programmes, we'll say the *Cosby Show*, that lots of young people watch where there's always a moral, where the children are always moral. They may behave slightly badly, but, by the end of the programme they've learnt the error of their ways. Why wouldn't people learn good things from television as well as this bad thing?

Mary Well of course... nobody's said otherwise. No, but you see the point about *EastEnders* or one of the points about *EastEnders* was that it was smack in the middle of family viewing time. And it wasn't us, it was the BBC that said, quote, 'Nothing unsuitable for children should be shown during family viewing time,' and what did you have in 'EastEnders'? You had rape, you had drugs, you had overdoses of pills and the lot!

Wogan But my point is, and Andrew perhaps, you can take up this as well, young people are *used to* television. Perhaps in the fifties it was a new thing. They know the conventions of it... they *know* it's not real, don't they?

Andrew Yes, I think they do, and I think also that, people's appetite for programmes that Mrs Whitehouse would object to is pretty limited. I mean, for example, in the United States, two of the channels that you can subscribe to, one is the Playboy channel, which I would have thought almost every programme Mrs Whitehouse would object to, and another is the Disney channel which we're bringing to Britain. The Disney channel, I would have thought contains programmes almost every one of which Mrs Whitehouse would love. It's a family entertainment channel. Now the Playboy channel has 400,000 subscribers in America and the Disney channel has 5 *million* subscribers in America. Playboy channel's going bust; the Disney channel is a great profit-maker.

Mary I think...

Wogan So there's no future for soft porn?

Andrew Well, I think people vote with their feet. See, part of the problem was in the days when Mrs Whitehouse was complaining about The Wednesday Play, people wouldn't vote with their feet; there really wasn't anywhere else to go. Maybe one other channel, at the most two...

Mary Well, there's ITV.

Andrew Well, maybe, one or two. That's not a huge choice compared to, say, the number of newspapers that are on sale every morning in this country. Everything from the *Sun* to *The Financial Times*. In days to come, with the huge channel choice that there's going to be, people will vote with their feet. If there's something that offends them, they'll switch to another channel. They will watch channels that don't offend them. Rather, I think, than having pressure groups of people, or the kind of people who run the BBC or ITV dictating to the rest of the public what's going to be on.

Mary Yes, but you see, there's a very important point here, I think. There are now internationally over 7... 800 cases now, 820 odd pieces of research internationally which show a link between televised and social violence. Now look, no, you laugh...

Andrew Well, you know, for every sociologist you get two opinions...

Mary No, no it isn't...

Andrew It's like, for every economist you get four opinions... Ah, you can produce... I mean, the one thing I do know, because there's been a lot of work done into this, is that, despite the millions of pounds spent on research, there is nothing conclusive to show a link between violence in society and violence on television.

from *Wogan*

These three letters were originally published on the Letters Page of the *Guardian*.

Little to be seen on TV through the eyes of a child

TEACHERS and parents know that Neighbours is at present the most popular programme with children of all ages from infants to sixthformers.

There is anecdotal evidence that during school holidays many children watch the same episode twice every afternoon. It is not our purpose to be critical of the quality of Neighbours, or to suggest that it may have a harmful effect on the young. We know that defining the excellence of a soap-opera and determining the kinds of influence it may have on its viewers are complex issues on which we do not feel able to express a confident view.

However we do question the appropriateness of transmitting this programme five days a week at peak viewing-time for children. We regard this as an opportunity missed – an opportunity for the BBC to call on its impressive range of talent to dramatise and serialise some of the absorbing and substantial children's fiction currently available. If the old Jackanory format is no longer considered feasible for storytelling, one has only to look at the recent success of Channel Four's Storyteller series to appreciate the exciting new possibilities for presenting folk and fairy tales. And what about poetry? It is alive and vigorous in schools – so why not on television? The dramatisation of The Lion, the Witch and the Wardrobe was an exciting and ambitious venture, but it has done nothing to fill the emptiness which precedes the weekday evening news on BBC1.

We would like to know if Anna Home, Head of BBC Children's Programmes, acknowledges that the Corporation has a responsibility to make appropriate provision for the millions of children – and adults with their children – who are the BBC's viewers at this important time in daily family life.

David Bridges, Jill Brown, Sally Crampton, Sandra Dunn, John Fish, Simon Hoad, Carole Lyne, Daphne A. Tucker, Victor Watson.
Homerton College, Cambridge

So that's why good Neighbours have become such good friends with the children

YOUR correspondents from Homerton College, Cambridge (Letters, January 11) suggest that the teatime episode of Neighbours should be replaced by a children's story. Their grounds for this appear to be that so many children watch Neighbours because of its transmission time – which, no doubt, has some validity – without acknowledging that it is the content of Neighbours that makes it compulsive viewing for millions of all ages.

Do these signatories watch Neighbours regularly? I do. And I think that Neighbours is probably more beneficial to many children (and to older people) than "good literature". People relate to it because it is a story of our time about everyday people, with everyday problems and how they cope with them.

Why are Oz soaps, in particular, so popular? For a start take the Oz soap Sons and Daughters: the title is a relationship, and the title Neighbours is a relationship. Compare these with English soaps Coronation Street and Emmerdale Farm which are impersonal place names. Does this reflect a basic difference between English and Australian culture?

I believe that the reason why Neighbours is so popular is because it provides a vision of something which is lacking from the lives of many people in England today; namely, a sense of personal commitment and caring in the community. A soap might appear to be merely a superficial time-filler to some people, but I am convinced that it goes far deeper than this.

Jane Carlisle.
Rochester, Kent

THERE is no question of any retreat from the BBC's responsibility to cater for the many millions of children who make up our audience and who watch our programmes as avidly as they watch Neighbours (Letters, January 11).

However, Children's BBC is scheduled between 3.50pm and 5.35pm on weekdays. The 5.35pm prenews slot in which Neighbours is shown marks the start of the main BBC1 peak time programming designed for the entire family. Within Children's BBC we have a strong drama strand on Wednesday at 5.10pm, currently the classic Tom's Midnight Garden by Philippa Pearce, which will be followed by an original drama series, Country Boy, written by a well-known children's author, Bernard Ashley. We have just finished a second series of Simon and the Witch based on the characters by Margaret Stuart Barry, meanwhile Grange Hill continues our drama commitment on Tuesdays and Fridays.

In addition, on Monday to Friday at 4.15pm from now until April there is "Jackanory"-type story telling, the stories include: Alice in Wonderland, Matilda by Roald Dahl and The Whipping Boy by Sid Fleischman. As far as poetry is concerned we had a new series for younger children before Christmas called A Bear Behind, which used a wide variety of poetry and verse, and we will certainly be making another series. Although I would always like to be in a position to make more home-produced drama and story telling, I feel that our audience is not currently being deprived.

Anna Home.
Head of Children's Programmes,
BBC Television

Guardian Letters,
January 1989.

This essay, written by a Sociology teacher as an example of discussion writing for her students, presents two sides in the debate about the effects of television on a young audience. Towards the end, she indicates her own viewpoint:

The television debate

'You're not watching any more *Neighbours*. . . . it's bad for you . . .'

'Instead of sitting in front of the television night after night, try reading for a change – it might improve your mind . . .'

**SCHOOL BULLY ATTACKS CHILD AFTER WATCHING
THE A TEAM...**

TEENAGE MORALITY DECLINES OWING TO SEX ON TV...

Comments and headlines like these are heard or read nearly every day in our society. They are put forward by parents, teachers, journalists, politicians of both the Left and the Right, as well as by more famous spokespeople like Mary Whitehouse. They are all reflections of the same basic proposition – that television has the power to influence our behaviour and attitudes in quite a dramatic way.

Critics on both the Right and Left of the political spectrum see clear differences in their viewpoints on television. On the *Right*, there is the view that television can encourage children – particularly those who are 'disturbed' or 'socially deprived' – to imitate the anti-social acts they see on television. In fact, researchers have found it difficult to prove a link between television violence and violent behaviour. But the belief that one causes the other is so universal that it is seen as 'common sense'. The Right also claim that watching television makes children mentally lazy, unimaginative and even prevents the brain from developing intellectually.

On the *Left*, critics are concerned about the way certain groups of people, such as women, Blacks, the unemployed, the disabled, or the elderly, are represented on television. They fear that television encourages stereotyped views of people like the bossy mother-in-law, the drug-pushing Black youth, or the dumb blonde. In their view, such stereotypes are a powerful way of reinforcing narrow, prejudiced views of other people – particularly the disadvantaged.

The approaches of both Left and Right share a number of assumptions. They regard television viewers as passive and unable to resist the effects of the media. Viewers – especially children – are seen as innocent and helpless 'victims', moulded by the negative force of television. They are uncritical viewers, unable to distinguish the 'fiction' of TV programmes from 'real life'.

Perhaps there should be a different picture of the viewer – this time as an active, conscious and powerful decision-maker. I would argue that children, like adults, should be seen as active users of the media, able to choose and question what they watch. They are able to distance themselves from what is shown and clearly separate fiction from reality.

Arguments about the effects of television appear to pivot around the more fundamental debate on the nature of people. To view people as essentially unable to control the effect of what they watch is, I suggest, inadequate and even insulting, based as it is on scanty evidence. Certainly more research, which places the viewer at the centre of the television experience, is needed.

Pauline Leonard

ACTIVITIES

Please read Techniques on pp.134-135, before starting these Activities.

How important is television really?

What is your view of the influence of television in our lives? Is it generally good or bad? In groups, discuss which of these statements you agree with and which you disagree with:

Now rank these statements in order of how truthful you feel each to be. Give 1 to the most truthful and 8 to the least truthful.

Compare your group's rankings with those made by the other groups.

Discussing a transcript

In groups of four, read the *Wogan* show transcript on pp.128-129. Does this transcript indicate a good or a bad discussion on the importance of television?

- TV makes you lazy and passive.
- TV broadens your mind and opens up new interests.
- TV stops conversation between members of a family.
- TV gives a narrow, stereotyped view of Black and Asian people.
- Most people can't distinguish good television from bad.
- Schools' television is more educational than normal lessons.
- Watching violence on TV is harmful.
- TV does not fairly represent the views of minority groups in society.

1. Prepare two readings in which each of you takes the role of a participant. In the first reading, aim to highlight the *good* points of the discussion; in the second, aim to highlight the *bad*. As you prepare, refer closely to Techniques on pp.134-135, which give advice on how to speak, listen and behave in each case.

2. Which of your two readings, 'good' or 'bad', is more accurately supported by the text of the transcript? Why do you think this? Take the more 'accurate' version and perform this before your class. Explain afterwards why you have interpreted the transcript in this particular way.

Letters to a newspaper

Read the letters to the *Guardian* on p.130, giving various points of view on the influence on children of the TV serial *Neighbours*.

1. In pairs, devise a chart on which you can record both the **benefits** and **harmful effects** of this, or any other TV serial, according to each letter writer. Add any points of your own where appropriate.

2. Think of any programme you watch and enjoy, which some might consider unsuitable for people of your own age. Imagine you are somebody who finds this programme offensive. Write a letter as if to a national daily newspaper, to protest about various aspects of the programme.

3. Imagine that *you* have read this letter of protest. Write a letter of your own, explaining why you feel that this programme *is* suitable for people of your age. (See pp.**199-200** for Formal letter writing.)

Discussion essay

Write a discussion essay based on *one* of the statements from the activity 'How important is television really?' (See opposite). Use a similar discussion essay format to 'The television debate' on p.131 which has this basic pattern:

	1	2	3
'THE TELEVISION DEBATE'	The Left's view	The Right's view	The author's view
YOUR ESSAY	Points FOR the statement	Points AGAINST the statement	Your view

You will need to find evidence to support the points you wish to make, both for and against the statement. Your evidence might be drawn from:

- your own experience of TV,
- the reading material in this chapter,
- discussion notes from the activity, 'How important is television really?'
- questionnaires/interviews with people in your class,
- scanning programming schedules like the *Radio Times* and *TV Times*.

TECHNIQUES

Discussing : in groups

GOOD

Aim:	What this means	DO	For example
CREATE UNDER-STANDING	A good discussion relies on the exchange of several views. Aim to cooperate with others and recognise their right to speak.	1. ENCOURAGE	• Ask quieter people to speak, and to explain their views. • Respond positively to other people, even if you do not agree with them.
		2. RELIEVE TENSION	• Lighten the mood with humour.
LISTEN WELL	If you listen well, you will hear and understand others better. You will hear a wider range of views. You will reach agreement more quickly, when needed.	1. USE BODY LANGUAGE	• Make eye contact with the speaker. • Nod, smile and look interested.
		2. SPEAK!	• Respond to people's comments with: 'Yes, I see...' 'Good point, but...'
SPEAK WELL	To be a good speaker, you need to be versatile: use a range of approaches when appropriate.	1. GIVE AND SEEK INFORMATION	
		2. BUILD	• Add to what other people are saying.
		3. QUESTION	• Query the truth of an assumption made to sound like fact.
		4. PROPOSE	• Suggest new ideas, points.
		5. ASSESS	• Weigh up the merits of your case and other people's.
		6. SUMMARISE	• Sum up your own case and other people's.

BAD

Aim not to:	What this means	DON'T	For example
CAUSE TENSION	A poor discussion is often caused by a self-centred person. Try not to compete or 'show off': this makes other people tense, and fewer viewpoints are expressed.	1. COMPETE	• Talk the most; show off; vie for attention.
		2. BULLY	• Be aggressive to others in order to assert yourself.
		3. FOOL AROUND	• Clown, joke.
		4. WITHDRAW	• Daydream, doodle, refuse to talk.
LISTEN BADLY	Poor listeners are usually people who prefer the sound of their own voice! You have two ears and one mouth, so listen twice as much as you speak!	1. DISTRACT	• Fidget, yawn, avoid eye contact, stretch.
		2. INTERRUPT	• Butt in, then immediately disagree.
SPEAK BADLY	Poor speakers speak too loudly and too often! Of course you must speak – ideally, each person should have an equal share of the time available. If you are shy, you may not speak enough, so practise!	1. ATTACK	• Criticise excessively.
		2. BLOCK	• Stop other people from making a point. • Talk over others. • Argue stubbornly.
		3. PLEAD	• Whine or whinge about a 'pet' concern.
		4. TAKE OVER	• Interrupt someone else, then take over the point s/he is making.

Assessing a group discussion

The Assessment Sheet opposite is for recording how people behave in a group discussion. It can be used by an observer to assess any group discussion activity in this book. It could also accompany the activity 'How important is television really?' on p.132.

> **The role of the observer**
>
> 1. You will observe (but not participate in) a group discussion.
> 2. Watch the way each person in the group behaves in discussion and record your observations on a copy of the Assessment sheet opposite.
> 3. Make sure that you are familiar with the qualities which make people good or bad in discussion. For this, study Techniques on pp.134-135.
> 4. To record your observations, tick the appropriate box on the chart each time a person displays one of the listed features.
> 5. At the end of your observation, put **x** in the boxes where a type of behaviour is not true of that person at all.
> 6. Notice whether a pattern of behaviour has emerged for each person you have observed.
> 7. Tell the class what your findings are. Describe the strengths and weaknesses of each person you observed. Explain why you felt the discussion was either successful or unsuccessful.

Experts' ranking for the desert survival exercise on p.127

1 Cosmetic mirror
2 Top coat
3 1 litre of water per person
4 Flashlight
5 Parachute
6 Jack-knife
7 Plastic raincoat
8 Pistol
9 Sunglasses
10 Compress kit
11 Magnetic compass
12 Air map
13 Vodka
14 Salt tablets

Nobody stranded in the desert should ever attempt to walk – dehydration is the main problem. Staying put, protecting yourself from the sun, and signalling your position are the best tactics.

Discussion assessment sheet

		Names:				
GOOD						
Create understanding						
Listen well						
Give/seek information						
Build						
Question						
Propose						
Assess						
Summarise						
BAD						
Cause tension						
Listen badly						
Attack						
Block						
Plead						

Date: Activity:
Group: Observer:

12 · Persuading

The sales assistant and the customer

Working in pairs, imagine that one of you is a sales assistant selling accessories in a department store. You get commission on every item you sell – without it your wages are very low. Your partner is a customer, looking for *one* of the items in the picture, but is not quite sure what colour/size/style s/he wants. Try to 'sell' this item to your partner, being as persuasive as possible. It is up to both of you whether a purchase is made or not.

Selling an object

Find something which you could 'sell' – a bag, an item of stationery, a book or bring something into the class that you would really like to sell! Then take a few moments to work out how you would:

- sell it on the doorstep,
- demonstrate it in a department store,
- advertise it on TV.

Then, in pairs or groups, try to 'sell' your object using at least *one* of these approaches.

To leave, or not to leave school

In pairs, take turns to be the person who persuades in these two situations:

1. You want to leave school at sixteen; a parent or friend tries to persuade you to continue your education.
2. You want to continue your education; a parent or friend tries to persuade you to leave.

Which of the two situations was the more realistic? Which of you was the more successful at persuading, and why?

Selling a good cause

Select *one* group in the class to carry out this exercise. Each person in the group should choose a different 'good cause' whose work you support – for example, an environmental or animal welfare group, a Third World charity, a local campaign.

Imagine that your class has decided it can afford to contribute to *one* of these good causes only. Each of you must prepare a case to persuade the class to support your 'good' cause rather than the others.

When each of you has made your case, ask the class to vote on which 'good cause' they feel most persuaded to support.

This poem by Christopher Marlowe was published in 1599, during the reign of Elizabeth I.

The Passionate Shepherd to His Love

Come live with me and be my Love,
And we will all the pleasures prove
That valleys, groves, hills, and fields,
Woods, or steepy mountains yields.

And we will sit upon the rocks
Seeing the shepherds feed their flocks,
By shallow rivers, to whose falls
Melodious birds sing madrigals.

And I will make thee beds of roses
And a thousand fragrant posies,
A cap of flowers, and a kirtle
Embroidered all with leaves of myrtle;

A gown made of the finest wool,
Which from our pretty lambs we pull;
Fair linëd slippers for the cold,
With buckles of the purest gold;

A belt of straw and ivy buds
With coral clasps and amber studs;
And if these pleasures may thee move,
Come live with me and be my Love.

The shepherd swains shall dance and sing
For thy delight each May morning:
If these delights thy mind may move,
Then live with me and be my Love.

Christopher Marlowe

This was written by a student as a parody of Marlowe's poem. She used the television serial *Star Trek* as her setting.

Flash Gordon to Dale Arden (or 'Beam Me Up Scottie')

Come fly with me, we'll boldly go,
and then we'll Klingons overthrow,
these great star-systems of the past
disintegrated with one blast.

    And we will swing upon the stars,
    and see the captains fight their wars
    by distant planets to whose lands,
    the odious Ming brings evil hands.

        And I will make you scores of rockets,
        and hundreds of electric sockets,
        a suit of silver and a spaceship,
        computerised with silicon-chip.

            A robot of the finest tin,
            which we may summon like a djinn,
            a thermal space coat for the cold,
            with lining of Venusian gold.

                A comet in a special box,
                with neutron clasps and laser locks.
                If these ideas don't cause you woe,
                Come fly with me, we'll boldly go.

                    The Martian men shall dance and sing
                    – for your delight – while on the wing.
                    If these delights your heart may woo,
                    then fly with me, we'll boldly go.

Love poem

Write a modern day version of Marlowe's love poem, making your version as persuasive as the original. You might use one of these ideas:

Come fly with me...
from: *a space pilot*
Come dive with me...
from: *a deep sea diver*
Come ride with me...
from: *a tandem cyclist*
Come climb with me...
from: *a mountain climber*
Come dance with me...
from: *a disco dancer*

A poem needs a form. Choose *one* of these approaches:

The chart single
Write your version of the love poem as a chart single, using free verse. For this, you do not need to use a special rhythm or rhyme pattern, unless it feels right to do so. You might consider setting your poem to the music of a pop song you know well. But make sure you keep as close as possible to the *content* of the original poem.

Parody of an Elizabethan poem
Write a modern version of Christopher Marlowe's poem, using the same rhythm and rhyme pattern as the original. Look at the *Star Trek* poem as an example.

The nymph's reply to the shepherd

A year after Christopher Marlowe wrote his poem, Sir Walter Ralegh responded with a poem in the same style. This is the first stanza:

> *If all the world and love were young,*
> *And truth in every shepherd's tongue,*
> *Those pretty pleasures might me move*
> *To live with thee and be thy Love.*

Continue Sir Walter Ralegh's poem, in which you explain why you must resist the shepherd's persuasions. Try, as far as possible, to write in the style of Marlowe and Ralegh. Aim to write each stanza as a reply to the stanza it corresponds to in Marlowe's poem. The tone of your poem should be light, mocking and 'down to earth'. (To remind you of the way rhythm and rhyme works, read 'Appreciating Poetry' on p.88.)

Reflection

After writing your version of an Elizabethan poem, discuss with a partner your responses to these questions:

- Which elements of Marlowe's poem have you tried to keep in your version?
- Which elements of the original have you changed?
- What did you find easy/difficult about writing your version of either the Marlowe or the Ralegh poem?

This publicity material comes from two charities which campaign for the welfare of homeless and unemployed young people. The letter on pp.143-145 is from the National Council of YMCA's; the hand-out on pp.146-147 is from Shelter.

Dear Friend,

Easter 1989

What's it like to be young today? - not one of the lucky ones, with a loving home and a belief in your own worth....but inexperienced, vulnerable and alone.

What was it like for <u>Susan</u>? It seemed as though 'life had it in' for Susan when we met her first.

Susan was just sixteen. She had no job. Her boyfriend was in prison. And when her parents found out she was going to have a baby, they threw her out.

Thank God Susan had the YMCA to turn to.

Susan had no home, no job, and her baby's father was in jail...

We gave her a roof over her head. And we gave her the advice and guidance she so desperately needed. A few months later Susan's lovely baby boy was born....and she began to make plans.

<u>Then the cruellest blow struck. Susan's baby died.</u>

The only mourners at that heartbreaking funeral were Susan and her friends from the YMCA.

We could see that Susan had lost the will to live. She stayed in her room....she lost weight with frightening speed....and slammed the door on every offer of help.

But gradually - very gradually - the sheer determination of the YMCA people around her, won. They helped Susan join a voluntary work scheme. She got a place on a training scheme....and finally a full-time job.

So Susan managed to climb back from the depths of despair - slowly at first - but with time she was on the path to being a happy young woman. She could enjoy life again, and live it to the full.

But how can you start believing in yourself if, like Mike, you've got no job, no money, no school qualifications worth mentioning – and you're disabled as well?

When Mike came to the YMCA's Training For Life, we could see he'd accepted the world's view of himself. On top of the difficulties shared by his group, Mike had a withered arm. With so little reason to feel good about life – and that's true of a great many young unemployed who we meet – Mike seemed to have lost any spark of interest.

Young people need training that's sensible, skilful and caring. That's why Mike benefited from the YMCA's Training for Life.

A printing works (which Mike liked) proved quite unsuitable. Office work just wasn't for him. And the kind of jobs that looked within his capacities always seemed to get filled by lads with two fit arms.

Mike had given up, we could see that. But the YMCA persevered.

We tried one last placement for him in the stores of a bathroom fittings manufacturer. To our delight, Mike took an interest. He wanted to know more about the purchasing and stores work to which he was introduced.

So can you imagine Mike's delight when, at the end of the placement, the company asked if he would join them – as a stores clerk. But I wonder if you can imagine how we felt?

Because we know that for every Mike there are hundreds more kids out there who need our help, and our experience.

Some of the difficulties these young people have to face are new. But most of the underlying problems aren't. Youngsters need to experiment, to test themselves out, to learn their own strengths and cope with their shortcomings.

And when the dreams founder, and their belief in themselves hits rock-bottom, they need friends who'll recognise their worth and help them back on their feet again.

That's something the YMCA has experience in. Nearly one hundred and fifty years' experience of working with young people, in fact.

So why don't more people know about what we do?

It came as a shock to the YMCA to discover that although we're very good at working with young people, we've not been very good at talking about it. And in today's world, you need to be.

That's why I'm writing you this letter, now. Because the bills have started getting much larger than we can cope with.

We've cut expenses to the bone. And we're anxiously looking to see what more we can cut down on. But there's a problem none of us really wants to face. **Which one of the many ways in which we're helping young people at the moment should we scrap?**

|| The cost of this letter is being kept as low as I can. Because when you think it can cost £25 to give a bed to a distressed youngster then I could not bear to waste money that might help young people. ||

So please, if you can, help the YMCA go on with its fight to give young people what they need: hope, a decent roof over their heads, and a proper sense of their own worth.

Whatever you send will be truly appreciated. By us. And by kids who may be vulnerable, in trouble, or in deep despair with no way out that they can see....until the YMCA reaches them.

God bless you.

Alison Tilbe

Alison Tilbe
for the YMCA's National Council.

P.S. *If by any chance you have already seen a copy of this letter, or do not feel able to respond, could you please pass it onto someone else who might be interested? The success of our appeal is vital for kids like Susan and Mike.*

pps. If you know a homeless or distressed young person, please tell us. We need to know. We want to help.

National Council of Y.M.C.As.
640 Forest Road, London E17 3DZ Telephone: 01-520 5599

To protect vulnerable young people's identities, models are used in photographs, and some details have been disguised. But the basic stories are true.

"I JUST NEED SOMEWHERE TO LIVE AND THEN I'D BE ABLE TO GET ON WITH MY LIFE"

The words of a young homeless person who came to Shelter for help.

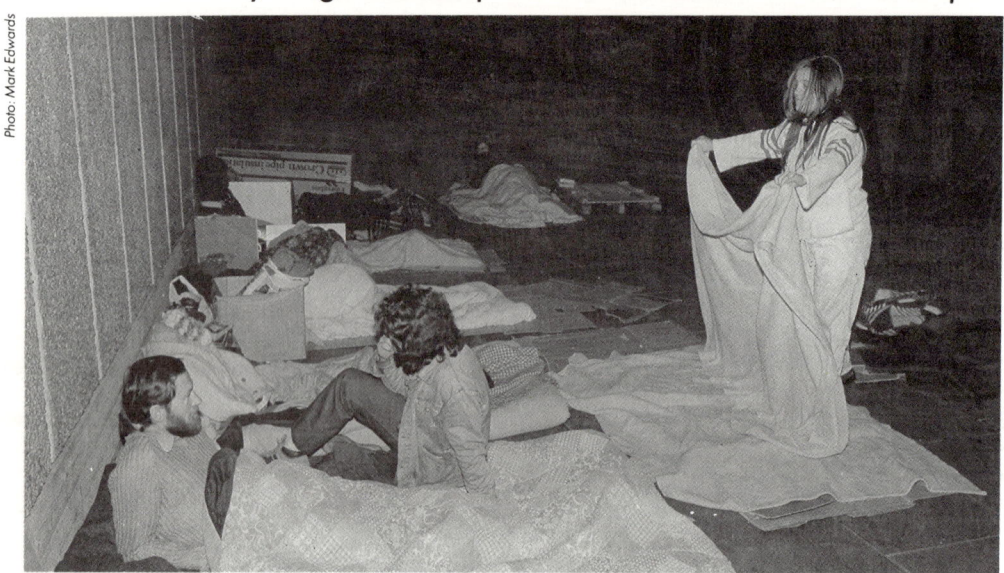

Photo: Mark Edwards

Young homeless people bedding down in London

Contrary to popular belief, young people become homeless for a variety of reasons. The stereotype of young homeless people as "vagrants, dossers, feckless and inadequate" implies that they are responsible for being homeless. Shelter's experience shows that most young people who come to us for help find themselves in circumstances which could affect anyone.

The vast majority of young people we see have one basic need, a decent home at a price they can afford. There is a difference, however, between identifying an immediate need, such as a roof for one night or for one week, and obtaining a long-term solution like a bed-sit, shared accommodation or even a place in a hostel.

YOUNG HOMELESSNESS
The hard facts

Shelter estimates that 80,000 young people experience homelessness every year.

In 1987 it was estimated that 25,000-40,000 young people were living rough in the London area.

A study of emergency night shelters has shown that 35% of young people interviewed had slept rough for at least one night; 71% of them were black.

Young homeless people are often told to return to their parents' home. This is not an option for many, particularly those who have just left care.

Why do young people leave home?

Most people leave their parental home by the age of 25. It is a natural process – a normal transition towards adulthood and independence. However, Britain's housing provision has not responded to this "acceptable process" and many young people therefore become "homeless". HOMELESSNESS IS A HOUSING PROBLEM, NOT A SIGN OF INADEQUACY.

One of the most disturbing trends among the young homeless is the disproportionate number who come from local authority care. There are many reasons why children are in the care of local authorities. Death or illness of parents, family homelessness, mistreatment or the desperation of parents. Whatever the reasons, it all adds up to intense, unavoidable distress for the child.

Being young and homeless is a vicious circle; it can often lead to unemployment which in turn makes finding a decent, permanent home very difficult.

In Shelter, we find the plight of young homeless people very disturbing. We have always committed ourselves to new work on behalf of these vulnerable members of our society. The extent of our activities depends on the committed concern and help of friends like you. The challenge to Shelter is enormous. Please help to help them by giving generously.

Shelter
NATIONAL CAMPAIGN FOR THE HOMELESS
88 Old Street · London EC1V 9HU · 01-253 0202

WHY SHELTER NEEDS £300,000

That is our target for this Christmas appeal. Because the challenge to Shelter is enormous.
- More young people are on the streets
- More people are homeless than ever before
- More people need Shelter's help and advice.
- We plan to open three new housing aid centres in 1989 in; Merseyside, Lincolnshire and Crawley

SHELTER'S HOUSING AID CENTRES EXPANSION

Shelter's Housing Aid Centres up and down the country are providing help and support for young homeless people, families and elderly people trapped and forgotten in wretched rooms and flatlets.

Our planned expansion of three new Centres will mean, that we can take on new workers who will provide the vital expert advice and support homeless people need.

Please add your support to our vital network of Housing Aid Centres with a Christmas gift.

"Homelessness for these young people means living on the streets or surviving in low quality housing and squats, in search of employment, it is evident that the restricted lifestyle of these young people damages their health and makes them vulnerable to economic exploitation and sexual abuse."

Taken from the Council of Europe symposium – International year of Shelter for the homeless

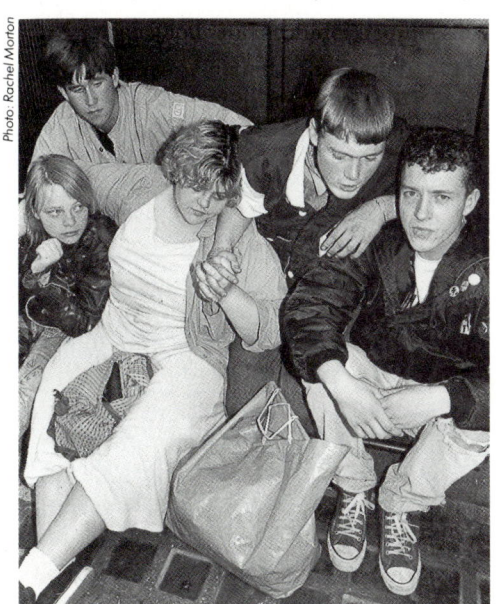

Young homeless people waiting outside a night shelter

Photo: Rachel Morton

How Shelter helps the young homeless

Because of constant disagreement at home, Simon was thrown out by his father. With nowhere to go he began living rough and during this time suffered from mental illness. As a result he was sectioned for 6 months in a mental hospital.

Towards the end of his time his aunt contacted Shelter to seek help in getting permanent housing. Shelter's case worker was able to negotiate with the local council and on Simon's discharge from hospital, a suitable offer of accommodation was made.

He is now living happily with his girlfriend in this accommodation and looks forward to a brighter future and better employment prospects.

Can no longer bear the abuse.

Mary B is a young girl, 17 years old. She left home and went to stay with friends when she could no longer bear the sexual abuse from her father. This had been going on for five years.

When she went to the council and applied as homeless, the council demanded evidence, that her father had sexually assaulted her before taking any action. "Evidence" in practice could have meant her going through the trauma of getting her father arrested in order to prove her case to the housing authority. It was only after our local advice centre and the Social Services Department intervened that the housing authority accepted responsibility for Mary placing her in temporary accommodation (where she can no longer be sexually abused) awaiting rehousing in another borough.

STOP PRESS Raise the roof – Shelter's most ambitious campaign to underline our determination to make a fuss – a big fuss – about the scandal of homelessness. We want people to sit up and take notice. And we want the government to do the same.

The message is simple. Homelessness is not an act of God, nor does it arise from the way people live.

Homelessness is due to the shortage of decent affordable accommodation.

We need to raise the roof to ensure that people have a better chance of being housed in the future.

Shelter
NATIONAL CAMPAIGN FOR THE HOMELESS
88 Old Street · London EC1V 9HU · 01-253 0202

Case study : Young people in need

Suppose that the YMCA and Shelter have decided to enlist the help of schools to support young people in need. They have asked you to design some publicity materials which may be used in a joint campaign called Young People in Need. The aim of this is to make pupils in secondary school aware of the problems faced by some young people, and of the work that the two charities do.

Work in groups both to prepare your thoughts and to design the publicity materials. You may find it helpful to study the Techniques section on pp.150-151 before you begin.

1. Preparing your thoughts
Read the case study material at least twice, then discuss the following:

1. What are the main needs of the people whom Shelter help?
   What are the main needs of the people whom the YMCA help?
2. Who or what is blamed for causing the problems of the young people helped by Shelter? By the YMCA?
3. Compare the ways in which Shelter and the YMCA provide help for young people.
   Do the two charities appear to offer similar or different long-term solutions to the problems faced by needy young people?
4. Do you feel that the two pieces of publicity have the same reader in mind? Which is the more suited to secondary school pupils?
5. How does each piece of publicity try to persuade the reader to support its cause? Compare the use of: ⟶
6. If you were to offer eight points of advice to someone designing publicity material for a charity, what would these be? For example:

> **text**: what is said
>   how it is said –
>   use of statistics,
>   personal
>   stories,
> **pictures**: how
>   these are used
> **captions**
> **headlines**
> **lay-out**: of text,
>   pictures,
>   captions and
>   headlines.

1. Always use a simple message such as: 'Homelessness is a housing problem, not a sign of inadequacy!' SHELTER

2. Designing the publicity

As a group, decide on your campaign approach. Look at all the tasks below and discuss what common features your campaign material will have. Consider the following:

aims
  what you wish to say,
message
  how you will say it,
name and logo
  of your campaign,
design elements
  colour, lettering, images, lay-out,
response
  what kind of support you want readers to give.

Then decide how the group will allocate work on these activities:

Poster

Design the rough lay-out and text for a poster (see p.**208**), on behalf of the YMCA and Shelter aimed at secondary school pupils. The rough message of the poster might be:

> *You are lucky – there are many young people who are not.*

or *You may not need our help today, but what about tomorrow?*

The poster should be designed so that it can be displayed on walls in communal spaces around the school. It should have a specific purpose – to raise money, to invite people to the tape-slide show (below), to sign a petition etc.

Article

Write an article of about 400 words in length to be placed in your school newspaper or magazine. Its main aim should be to persuade pupils to support the campaign. You might do this by outlining:

- the problems faced by some young people; why these problems come about,
- the work carried out by the two charities; why this is so important,
- the aims of the campaign;
- the role of your own school in helping to design publicity materials,
- the role your readers might play in supporting the campaign – by giving a few pence, signing a petition etc.

Script/storyboard

Draft the script and storyboard (see pp.**203-204**), for a tape-slide show which you intend to show to the first-years in your school. Your storyboard should aim to cover the same information as the newspaper article above. Both script and storyboard should make these points more simply and imaginatively, without upsetting younger children.

TECHNIQUES

Persuading

When you are trying to persuade a person to do something, you may be appealing to two sides of their nature.

Love, Compassion, Guilt, Greed, Selfishness

Understanding, Questioning, Logic, Judgment

There are various methods of persuading which may appeal to a person's emotions. These include:

Method	Example (from YMCA letter)
Personal stories	Susan was just sixteen. She had no job. Her boyfriend was in prison. And when her parents threw her out...we gave her a roof...cruellest blow struck...climb back from the depths of despair...and live it to the full.
Direct appeal or plea	But how can you start believing in yourself if, like Mike, you've got no job, no money, no school qualifications worth mentioning — and you're disabled as well? So, please, if you can, help the YMCA go on with its fight...
Emotive language	...inexperienced, vulnerable, alone. ...Susan's lovely baby boy was born and she began to make plans. Then the cruellest blow of all. Susan's baby died. She stayed in her room...she lost weight with frightening speed...and slammed the door on every offer to help.

If you want a person to 'see reason' the main approach is by arguing a case:

Method	Example (from Shelter hand-out)
Explaining your case	*Contrary to popular belief, young people become homeless for a variety of reasons.* *The vast majority of young people we see have one basic need, a decent home at a price they can afford.*
Supporting with facts	*Most people leave their parental home by the age of 25.* *In 1987 it was estimated that 25,000–40,000 young people were living rough in the London area.*

Supporting with quotations	*"I just need somewhere to live and then I'd be able to get on with my life."*
	      (A homeless young person)
	
	"Homelessness for these young people means living on the streets…"
	      (Council of Europe symposium)

Questioning stereotypes	*The stereotypes of young homeless people as 'vagrants, dossers, feckless and inadequate' implies that they are responsible for being homeless. Shelter's experience shows…*
Stating your message	*HOMELESSNESS IS A HOUSING PROBLEM, NOT A SIGN OF INADEQUACY.* *Please give generously.*

- In rough, write a short persuasive letter on behalf of a charity or campaigning group you support, to be sent to members of the public. Aim to use as wide a range of the persuasive methods listed above, as possible. When you have finished, ask a partner to identify the methods you have used. How might the letter be improved?

13 · Arguing

STARTERS

Having a row

One definition of 'arguing' is 'having a row'. Imagine that you have done something which has really angered a friend. Your friend comes over to you and starts an argument with you. In pairs, choose from these opening lines:

'Where's my record? You promised to bring it back today...'
'How dare you! You promised not to tell anyone...'
'Why didn't you turn up last night? I was waiting...'
'When are you going to pay me back? It's six days now...'

Take turns to try out these two approaches:
- react angrily to your friend's accusations.
- be calm and reasonable with your friend.

Which approach is more natural to you? Which is better?

Arguing a case

Another definition of 'arguing' is 'making a case for something'. There are many things in life people want but can't get. Suppose a reasonable adult has said to you, 'I'll consider it, if you argue your case.' Work out your case for one of these wishes:

- more pocket money,
- staying out later,
- having your own door key,
- having a specialist piece of equipment,
- taking a job,
- going to stay with a friend.

Take turns to put your case to the 'reasonable adult'.

Bee in your bonnet

Arguing can also mean 'debating an issue' you feel strongly about. It might be a 'pet hate' or it might be a political point of view:

- travelling to and from school,
- examinations,
- troops in/out of Northern Ireland,
- vivisection/ bloodsports/zoos,
- school dinners/ uniforms/length of the day,
- YTS schemes,
- Welsh language/ Scottish parliament,
- smoking.

In groups, 'sound off' about your viewpoint, beginning with the line: *'Listen to me for a minute will you?...'*
Immediately after this, someone from the group should try to answer your case from the opposite point of view.

SHOULD THIS RABBIT BE

YES

Margaret Franklin and Mark Matfield of the Research Defence Society

Isn't it marvellous when lives are saved thanks to modern surgery?

With transplants, those in pain and suffering can return to a normal life. Because of vaccines, killer diseases like diphtheria, polio, smallpox and tuberculosis have been beaten. Hip joint replacements can transform a cripple to an active person, while women in childbirth are no longer at great risk thanks to drugs which control fatal infections. Insulin prevents over three million diabetics from suffering a slow, wasting death.

All this has been made possible because of research on animals. Without animal experiments, little Ben Hardwick, who captured the nation's heart when he needed a liver transplant, would have had no hope of a life-saving operation. But there was not one word in all the publicity about the scientists who pioneered the treatment, using animal research.

It is fashionable today to criticize modern drugs and the ways that we develop them, but we should never forget that there have been millions of lives saved by them.

Animals themselves benefit from animal research. Animal experiments are needed to produce the veterinary medicines which save animal lives. Remember Sefton, the cavalry horse who was so badly injured in an IRA bomb blast? He was restored to good health by veterinary surgeons, using techniques developed in animal experiments.

We should also remember that much animal testing is required, by law, for our own protection, testing drugs to make sure they are safe before being tried in human beings. One tragic case where a drug was not properly tested on animals was Thalidomide, which was not tested in pregnant animals before being prescribed to humans. We all know the heart-breaking results that caused. Animals are the best models we have for human beings. They are not ideal – no model ever is – but they are a much better model than anything else available.

A new drug has to be tested on an entire body system. Carrying out the same tests on a tissue sample in a test tube simply does not give the same results. That is why animal experiments are so important. A great deal of research is done to develop non-animal 'alternative' methods but, because they are so different from animals, progress is very slow.

Because it is necessary to use animals in medical research, we have to make sure that they are treated as humanely as possible. In Britain we have the strictest laws in the world controlling animal research. When usable alternative methods are found, our law makes it illegal not to use them. When animals are used, they have to be fed, cared for and looked after very carefully.

Special permission from the government is required for all animal research. The scientist has to show that the research is important enough to use animals, that only the minimum number of animals are being used and that they will not suffer if it can be prevented in any way. The vast majority of the animals used in research are rats and mice. Sometimes it is necessary to use larger animals such as dogs, cats or primates, but first the scientist has to show that the research could not be done using rodents. That is why the use of these larger animals only amounts to a fraction of one percent of animal experiments in this country.

There has been a steady reduction in the number of animal experiments over the past decade because of these controls. Many animal experiments now involve no pain or discomfort for the animals, with no more being involved than a small injection or taking a blood sample. Anaesthetics are given for any surgical procedure, with post-operative pain killing drugs, as they would be given to a human being.

For those – fortunately very few – who break the rules, the penalties are severe. Not only could they be fined heavily but they could have their licence to work with animals removed, which might well end their career as a medical researcher.

Many universities and colleges have ethical committees which monitor their work. As well as answering to the law, scientists must answer to their fellow professionals.

If we are ever going to cure cancer and conquer AIDS, animal research will continue to be necessary for the foreseeable future.

'Animals benefit from animal research'

USED IN EXPERIMENTS?

NO

Jan Creamer, general secretary of the National Anti Vivisection Society

Vivisection doesn't work. Quite simply, the results of animal experiments cannot be applied successfully to human beings – history has proved it. The introduction of blood transfusions was delayed for more than 200 years by misleading results in animal experiments.

Chloroform, a useful anaesthetic in people, actually kills dogs, while morphine, often used as a tranquilliser, sparks wild excitement in cats and mice.

And Florey, the man who purified penicillin, always said it was a lucky chance he didn't test it on guinea pigs as it kills them.

So, you see, it is nonsense to suggest that experiments are necessary to make strides forward. They can actually be dangerous in producing misleading results.

The simple fact is animals aren't like us, they suffer from different diseases – and diseases they're given that are made in a laboratory aren't the same as the real world.

The inhumanity to animals is appalling. In one test, an animal, usually a rabbit, has a chemical product such as hairspray or an industrial cleaner, dripped into its eye to see how much it irritates it. No pain relief is given. It goes on for up to seven days while scientists study the ulceration, bleeding and swelling. We think it's outrageous to inflict such suffering. What's worse is that the test doesn't prove very much as a rabbit's eye is physiologically and structurally different to a humans.

The other disgraceful waste of life is the "safety" test when animals are force-fed a substance like weedkiller and detergent to find out how much is needed to kill them. It can last up to 14 days.

And what does that prove? Water can be lethal if you pump enough into a creature. You simply overload the system until it collapses.

We want to see this kind of useless experimentation banned.

Many advances have been made in medicine without using animals.

Contrary to the stories told, insulin, the life-saving drug for diabetics, was purified for use by a chemist without using animals.

Scientists have made us believe that drugs cure so many illnesses, but epidemics of diseases like diphtheria were on the wane before antibiotics came in. It was the leaps ahead in levels of health and hygiene that eradicated them.

In the research to find drugs to cure cancer, much of the testing is done on mice. But mice suffer a different kind of cancer to humans. They tend to suffer from sarcomas, affecting bones and tissues, while humans get carcinomas, occurring in covering membranes.

And the cancers induced in a laboratory grow quite differently from natural cancers – so the treatment can have a different effect. The tests cannot be conclusive.

Drugs must go through clinical tests on human beings before they are available to the public anyway. We say that any experiments carried out before that point are completely invalid. It's the reaction in humans that counts, and that alone.

So experiments on animals cause as many problems as they may one day prevent – and we don't believe the wonder drug that

'Experiments are inhuman and cruel'

scientists are constantly seeking will ever be found. We don't believe we should exploit animals for our own ends. They have no-one to speak out for them.

We fund medical research that doesn't torture animals and we've made quite a significant contribution to medical progress, including the bid to understand cot deaths.

And we've proved there are viable alternatives. We developed experiments on the human placenta – an ideal substitute for animals – and there are thousands of them thrown away every year.

More and more young people are coming round to our idea. In fact, our "Violence Free Science" campaign – run to give students the right to refuse to take part in dissection of animals in classes – has been one of the most successful ever.

Many pupils and students find the whole business of cutting up animals extremely disturbing. And it's the first step on the road to making them accept that these atrocities take place, without question. They become the vivisectors of the future.

Our bid to stop vivisection is based on scientific evidence. We've got plenty of it now.

Experiments on animals are as unproductive as they are inhuman and sickeningly cruel. We think the suffering should end. ■

from *Woman's Own*

Is private education a good thing? The 'Fact sheet' from *ISIS* argues the case for private education; the essay by sixth form student, Hélène Smith, argues the case against it.

INDEPENDENT SCHOOLS INFORMATION SERVICE
56 Buckingham Gate, London SW1E 6AG   01-630 8793/4

MYTHS ABOUT INDEPENDENT SCHOOLS

Opponents of independent education constantly use myths in the campaign to weaken and destroy independent schools. The facts are different.

Myth No 1: Independent schools are socially divisive
Independent schools do not create social divisions in society. They reflect them, just as comprehensive schools reflect them. The children attending independent schools come from all social and economic backgrounds.

The abolition of independent schools would not remove social division in education. It would simply increase inequalities within the maintained sector. Differences between schools in the suburbs and those in inner cities are often more marked than those between independent and maintained schools.

Myth No 2: Independent schools have an "Old Boy" network which provides a passport to privilege and power
This may well have been true in the past. Times, however, have changed. Entry to the professions is increasingly dependent on graduate qualifications. Independent school pupils have to compete on merit for jobs in today's competitive labour market. As for passing on privilege from one generation to the next, the fact is that at least 60 per cent of children come from families where the parents themselves did not attend independent schools.

Myth No 3: Independent schools have a back door to Oxbridge
This is a myth. Oxford and Cambridge Universities have given up reserving places for students from independent schools. Benefactors over the centuries have left money for colleges to provide funds for deserving pupils from certain independent schools, but the funds (now very small) are only available to pupils who win places on merit.

Myth No 4: Independent schools damage the maintained sector by diverting able children and teachers
Such an accusation is an insult to the maintained sector. More than half the independent schools in this country are comprehensive in the sense that they do not select children according to their ability. They specialise in helping children of average and below average ability to do their best. The vast majority of teachers, whether in the maintained or independent sectors, are able and dedicated. Those who work in the independent sector do so out of choice.

Myth No 5: Independent schools divert resources from the maintained sector
This is ludicrous argument. It has been estimated that independent schools <u>save</u> the maintained sector.£750 million a year, at a time when there are tight restraints on the public purse.

Independent schools receive some public funds, (i.e. £75 million in the form of boarding school allowances and £34 million on the assisted places scheme), but this is a particularly cost-effective use of such money and the amounts are insignificant compared with the savings.

Myth No 6: Independent schools' results are no better than those of comprehensives
Nearly 65 per cent of pupils at independent schools pass one or more A levels, compared with 13 per cent at comprehensive schools. Independent schools have 17 per cent of all sixth-form pupils and gain 25 per cent of all A level passes. A survey of schools in 1986 showed assisted places pupils achieving a 90 per cent pass rate in A levels, with an average of 3.2 per pupil and 54 per cent at A or B grades.

Private education is wrong

'The idea that differences of educational opportunity among children shall depend on differences of wealth among parents, is a barbarity.'
(R. H. Tawney)

There are many reasons why private education is wrong in my view, but this statement of principle stands out among them. In a democratic society like our own, there should be no segregation of colour, culture, religious belief, or wealth. I believe the way to achieve this is through education. It was Karl Marx who made the famous statement, *'From each according to his abilities to each according to his needs'*. If an egalitarian society is to be achieved, everyone should have the chance to develop to the best of their ability, regardless of their ability to pay.

Private education is socially divisive. It takes children who are privileged in various ways and places them in separate schools. From an early age, children in both the state and the private sectors are getting a false impression of the society they live in. Children in private schools are made to feel special, privileged, and even superior to their peers in state schools. Surely part of the point of education is to learn how to socialize with people of different religions, sexes, races, cultures and social classes? Without this people develop narrow-minded and prejudiced views about people who are different.

This social division does not stop within the schools. At the two most prestigious universities, Oxford and Cambridge, 58% of people accepted are privately educated. Yet only 7% of schools in this country are private! Whatever the reason behind this – the big emphasis in private schools on preparing for exams, or the system of specially reserved places for privately educated pupils – the result is the same. The privileged in our society are favoured.

After leaving school and university, privately educated people move on to the top jobs. At the moment, 80% of our judges, 89% of Navy admirals, 86% of generals, and 60% of Tory MPs were educated in private schools. Most of the editors of our newspapers come from private schools. The 'old boy network' continues to command our society, because the privileged classes always put their own interests first.

It seems extraordinary to me that, on top of all these advantages, private schools should receive money from the state. Labour Party statistics show that the full subsidy going to private education runs at well over £179 million. This is utterly scandalous when you consider that state schools are suffering from dilapidated buildings, lack of teachers and poor resources.

It is often argued in defence of private schools that they offer parents 'freedom of choice' in education. To take this freedom away, it is claimed, will remove one of our democratic rights.

But what is this 'freedom of choice'? The vast majority of people cannot afford private education. Do not tell me that 'poor' people can 'scrimp and scrape' to send their children to such schools: for many, 'scrimping and scraping' would not buy one week at such a school. Freedom of choice is for the well-to-do only, not for the poor.

   In my view, all private schools in this country should be closed. It should be made illegal for schools to charge fees for education. I would like to see the community as a whole agreeing the place of each school within the system and running all the schools in the public interest. Eton and Harrow could become hostels for homeless people. Schools would be the property of the local community and not reserved for the wealthy elite. This would be the only truly just solution.

Hélène Smith

Discussion and understanding

*Read the **ISIS** 'Fact sheet' and the essay on private education on pp.157-158. Also read Techniques on pp.162-163. Then in pairs, discuss and draft answers to these questions.*

1. The *ISIS* 'Fact sheet' mentions six myths. What is the original meaning of the word 'myth'? What does 'myth' mean here?
Note down any of Hélène Smith's statements which *ISIS* might describe as 'myth'.
Note down any 'facts' given by the *ISIS* sheet which Hélène Smith might describe as 'myth'.

2. How do *ISIS* and Hélène Smith each argue their point of view?
Are their methods of argument similar or different?
To answer this, note down the methods of argument used by both the 'fact sheet' and the essay on a chart like this one:

	ISIS	Hélène Smith
Similarities	Statements of opinion 'Independent schools do not create social divisions in society.'	Statements of opinion 'Private education is socially divisive.'
Differences		

3. Which argument do you find the more persuasive, the one by *ISIS* or the one by Hélène Smith? Why do you think this?

4. Do you think that either of the two arguments has omitted any key points? If so, what are they?

Writing : *A bee in my bonnet*

Choose a controversial issue on which you have a clear opinion. (See the lists of topics on both p.153 and p.160.) Give your point of view either in essay form, or in the form of a fact sheet.

Case study : Argue your case!

For this case study, you will need access to, and a working knowledge of, a video camera. Also see Techniques on pp.162-163.

Imagine that a regional television company has invited members of your class to contribute to a ten minute programme for young people called, 'Argue Your Case!' This programme aims to use young people in all the main functions of programme making: to participate in the argument; to present the programme; and to help produce and film it.

The programme presents a different topic each week, chosen for its power to generate a lively argument. The presenter puts questions to three young people with conflicting views, and encourages debate amongst them. Programmes aim to be provocative and controversial. By the end, however, the presenter encourages the guests to reach some measure of agreement.

1. Selecting a topic
As the team of five chosen to make a programme, select *one* topic which interests all of you. At least two of you should have strong views on this topic – one for and one against – which you are prepared to express. Here is a suggestion list:

- capital punishment
- poll tax
- equal opportunities for women
- leaving school at sixteen
- private education
- vivisection
- nuclear disarmament

2. Doing research
As a team, aim to be as knowledgeable as possible about your chosen topic. Together, work out what you consider to be the case for each point of view. Then discuss how to find out more. Use your library to find out the addresses of campaigning groups, who might be able to send you free publicity arguing their case. (See p.**199** for writing formal letters.) Also look for library books and school videos on your topic.

3. Preparing your roles
Now choose the roles each of you would like to adopt while making the programme. Read the brief description of these roles at the top of p.161.

Presenter	You are responsible for the ultimate success or failure of the programme. You should:	**Opposer**	You are *against* a point of view. Carry out the same work as the Proposer.
	• decide how you will introduce and conclude the programme, perhaps writing out cue cards or a script to help you;	**Mediator**	**Either,** you have a balanced point of view – you see merits and problems on both sides of the argument. **Or** you have an alternative point of view – another way of looking at the topic. Carry out the same work as the Proposer.
	• work out challenging comments and questions to ask each person taking part;		
	• devise ways of encouraging agreement amongst the participants, before the programme ends;	**Producer/ Camera Operator**	You direct and advise on presenting the programme, working closely with the presenter; operate the video camera; run a technical rehearsal in which you work out timing, the opening shots, seating arrangements, camera angles and closing shots. Seek technical advice from somebody familiar with video, on the best shots to use in this kind of debate.
	• keep a careful check on timing;		
	• check p.134 on what makes a good/bad discussion.		
Proposer	You are *for* a point of view. You should:		
	• research into the subject in some depth;		
	• prepare rough answers to questions you may well be asked, using a range of arguing techniques (check p.162);		
	• be able to argue your point of view before an audience.		

4. Recording
If the team is well prepared, the video recording should go smoothly. When you are performing, try to forget the camera. Remember, this is not a rehearsal – you can't say, 'Can we do that bit again?' Invite the rest of your class to watch you while you record.

5. Assessing
At another lesson, watch the video recording each group has made. You might make an assessment of how effectively each participant has argued his or her case. To do this, draw a chart like the one on the right, and use the arguing techniques from p.162, as your criteria. Tick the appropriate box each time a participant argues in a particular way. The wider the spread of ticks on your chart, the more versatile the person arguing is likely to be.

	Julie	Saheed	Martin	Asha
Starting message	✓✓✓	✓	✓✓✓	
Starting opinion		✓✓✓	✓✓	✓	✓✓✓
Rhetorical question	✓✓			✓

TECHNIQUES

Arguing

The exercises in this section are based on *'Should this rabbit be used in experiments?'* on pp.154-155.

Whatever the reason you may have for arguing a case, there are methods of arguing we all use in common. Whether it is an argument with a friend, a class discussion, a debate or a letter of protest to a newspaper, you will use some of the approaches below:

Stating your message
When you argue a case, your audience or reader needs to know what your standpoint is. So state your message early on in a clear and succinct way. Then people will pay more attention to your argument.

- Look at the 'Yes' and 'No' arguments on vivisection. Do both state their message early on? Find the first example you can find from each article.

Stating your opinion
Arguments are usually about opinions, beliefs or feelings, rather than facts. It is quite common to interpret the same facts from opposing points of view – the *interpretation* causes the argument. It is also common for arguments to confuse fact with opinion, so that it is difficult to distinguish between them.

- Look at these three statements below. Two statements are opinions and one is a fact. How can you tell which is which?

  '...We don't believe we should exploit animals for our own ends...'
  '...Many universities have ethical committees which monitor their work...'
  '...Vivisection doesn't work...'

- Which of the above statements confuses fact with opinion?
- What might be the advantages, and the disadvantages, of doing this?

Rhetorical questions
It is quite common in an argument to ask a question which does not expect an answer. Look at these examples from 'Yes':

  '...Isn't it marvellous when lives are saved thanks to modern surgery?...'
  '...Remember Sefton, the cavalry horse injured in an IRA blast?...'

- What might be the value of asking rhetorical questions in an argument?

Emotive language

If you want to convince people of a point of view, emotive language may influence their feelings. Study the wording of these examples:

'... One tragic case where a drug was not properly tested on animals was Thalidomide. We all know the heart-breaking results that caused ...

'... We think it's outrageous to inflict such suffering ...'

- Which words have been chosen for their ability to sway people's emotions in these examples?

Attacking misconceptions

Crucial to arguing is the task of criticising the viewpoint of your opponent. If you feel strongly about your own view, you probably consider that your opponents have failed to understand the issue, or have misinterpreted the facts. Look at these two examples:

'... It is fashionable today to criticize modern drugs and the ways that we develop them, but we should never forget that there have been millions of lives saved by them ...'

'... So, you see, it is nonsense to suggest that experiments are necessary to make strides forward ...'

- Which words indicate here that the opponent has 'got it wrong'?

Giving evidence

It is unlikely that you will convince someone else of your point of view, without firm evidence.

'Evidence' usually means factual information which has been recorded or measured, such as statistics, quotations from people in authority and case histories

- Work through both the 'Yes' and 'No' articles, noting down all the instances of evidence used by each side. Which has the more impressive range of evidence in your view?

14 · Campaigning

National campaigns

1. In groups, think of ten national campaigns to add to this list:

2. Run a 'brainstorm session' in your group on all the ways in which a national campaign might publicise its issue. Think of typical ways and untypical ways. Draw up a list of thirty suggestions. Then share your ideas with the class.

Campaign group
Friends of the Earth
ASH

Issue
A better environment
A ban on smoking

Campaign display

1. In your group, choose *one* national campaign group in which you are all interested. Then write a letter to its headquarters, requesting any free publicity it might provide. (Use a reference book listing all campaigning groups, obtainable from most libraries, to look up the address.)
2. When all the groups in the class have received their publicity material, hold a Display Day when each group sets up a 'stall' and publicises their chosen campaign. Consider dressing up, preparing hand-outs, making a simple banner. The aim would be to encourage other people in the class to take an interest in your campaign.

Local campaigns

Is there a school or local issue you feel is important enough to campaign about? For example:

In groups, take one of these issues (or one similar). Think of ten ways to publicise and gain support for your cause.
Then put these in order of importance.
When you have done this, appoint a spokesperson for the group to present your campaign strategy to the class.

School
school uniform
length of school day
compulsory games

Local
poor youth facilities
housing developments
cleaner, safer streets

The reading materials which follow are taken from a real-life, local campaign. The map, the artist's impression and the names of people and places are fictitious.

Holt Protest Group

Dear People of Holt,

URGENT
YOU MUST READ THIS!

WHY? Your way of life in a community, your children's schooling, your use of local roads and paths, and the value of your house will be at risk if 2,000 houses are built at Holt by Green Lands Ltd.

A reminder of who we are, because there are many new householders in the area who will not have heard of us. The Holt Protest Group was formed when it became known that Green Lands were planning to build a vast new housing estate on the country boundary of Holt.

So please join us. Let's try to stop Green Lands getting planning permission to ruin our lives. Holt may be just a modern suburb on the outskirts of a large city. But many of us moved here in the first place to get away from the dirt and noise of inner city life.

We want the voice of Holt to be heard. We live here, so we will be most directly affected. Do we want our home environment to be destroyed? Just to make profits for developers? *If we do not make our position known, no one else will.*

What are the grounds for our protest? First we feel Holt has grown quickly enough as it is. From a population of 5,000 to 10,000 in under seven years. Are we now expected to absorb another 6,000 or more people? Surely it is time to rest, to allow our own community to find its feet? A new estate of 2,000 houses sounds like a mini-town in itself and yet it is to be made part of Holt!

Second, it will put a huge pressure on Holt. The roads would become even more noisy and congested with traffic. There would be parking problems at Holt shopping centre and railway station. Community facilities always lag behind the building of houses and these will soon become inadequate.

Third, what about our children? The proposed new road leading to the housing estate will have to cut right through the school grounds. High fences cannot stop the noise or danger of constant traffic rushing past. Perfectly good sports fields will be laid under tarmac. Our children will be forced to walk over a mile to the new sports site, and back again. What price, their education?

Last, the reason we all moved to Holt – the countryside nearby – will disappear under bricks and mortar. Forget Green Lands' promises of screening – our view of the countryside will go.

NOW is the time to make a stand for the fields and woodland, the wild animals, birds, butterflies and flowers and the views. NOW is the time to fight, so we may preserve the lung which recreates us at the end of the day and week; here, where we want to bring up our families.

The price of our freedom is vigilance. We must fight this, every inch of the way. Do not be taken in by seductive gestures, like a health centre or a swimming pool. Remember the wise Trojan's words from the *Iliad* in the wooden horse saga, "I fear the Greeks – even bearing gifts!"

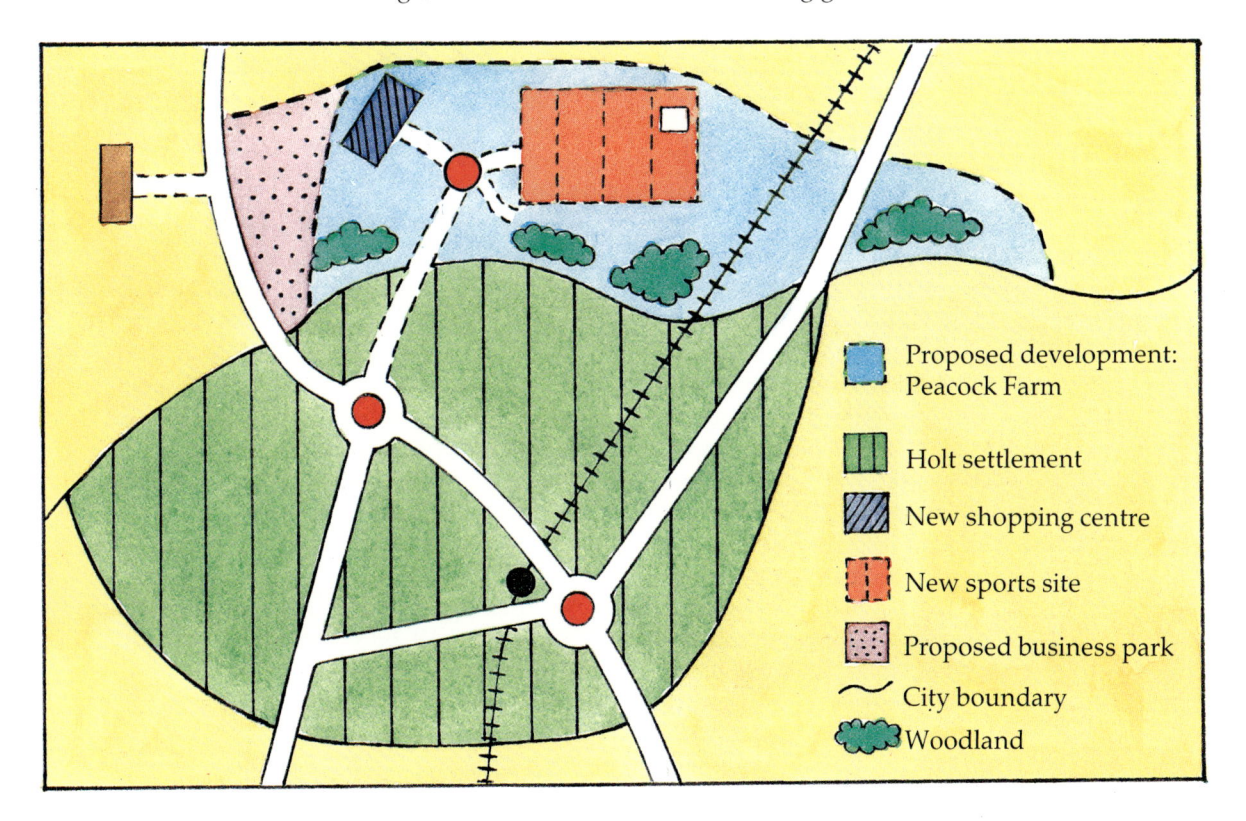

Please come to:
 AN OPEN MEETING FOR EVERYBODY
 TO DISCUSS PEACOCK FARM
 AT HOLT COMMUNITY CENTRE
 ON _____

Whatever your view, we hope to see you there.

Yours sincerely,

J Smithson

John Smithson
Chairman, Holt Protest Group.

"WE WILL WIN!" says developer

Huge benefits are in store for the local community if Green Lands Ltd get the go-ahead for Peacock Farm, the planned new housing estate in Holt.

Famous for its reputation as a 'caring' developer, Green Lands Ltd will be building houses with environmental conservation in mind. All houses, whether 'starter homes' or 'executive', will be built from local, natural materials. All will have special wall and loft insulation and buyers will be given the option of solar heating panels.

Concern for the environment will not stop at your front door. Two woodland sites will be designated 'conservation areas', and community spaces will be provided for bottle, waste paper and aluminium 'banks'.

Public open space will be generous and plentiful on the 500 acre site. After 950 houses have been built 52 acres will be handed over; after 1,550 houses another 24 acres, and after 2,000 houses, 19 acres.

Additionally, there will be a further 95 acres for smaller pieces of open space such as adventure playgrounds. Four acres of land will be available at cost for housing association land.

A massive £160,000 will go on woodland maintenance, and £100,000 will be given to improve footpaths, cycle paths, and the environment three miles round the new estate. Careful landscaping and planting of trees will ensure that there are natural screens between Peacock Farm and the rest of Holt.

From the time the very first house is built, £100,000 will be donated to improve car parking in Holt itself. A massive £1 million will be contributed to Holt Health Service. A Health Centre will be donated as will a community hall with car parking.

Holt's secondary school will also benefit. The school is to get a brand new sports site providing playing fields, tennis courts and a swimming pool. These facilities will be available to both Holt and Peacock Farm residents during the evenings and at weekends.

Although the benefits to the community are considerable, a spokeswoman for Green Lands Ltd said they did not stop

An artist's impression of the shopping centre proposed for Peacock Farm.

there. "What these protesters don't realise", she said, "is that we are developing the new estate for the benefit of the whole of Holt. The people who object the loudest are probably the very ones who will most benefit. There will be more jobs for local people while the estate is being built. Then there will be permanent jobs in the new business park. Holt's shopkeepers will get more trade and there will be better community facilities for families.

"These protesters are being hypocritical. We're building houses for people just like them. People who want to get out of the city centre and live the good life near the country. People who are single or newly married and want to buy their first home. Families, wanting something bigger. We will be building for all needs.

"The way these protesters think is 'What is good for us, isn't good for anyone else'. Well, we want to change that."

from *Holt and District Gazette*

ACTIVITIES

Discussion and understanding

Read the material on pp.166-169 carefully. Then in pairs or groups, discuss the questions below, to prepare you for the case study on the next page.

If campaigns are to succeed, they must be persuasive. Effective persuasion appeals both to people's emotions and to their reason. Look at the methods of persuasion on the right. Also see Techniques on p.150 for more details.

1. Check that you understand the meaning of the terms in the box.
2. Find examples of each persuasive method, if it is used, in both the letter and the article.
3. Are there any other persuasive methods used which are *not* mentioned in the box?
4. Compare the similarities and differences between the methods of persuasion used by the protesters and by the developers, like this:

The emotions
Personal stories
Direct appeal or plea
Emotive language

Reason
Explaining your case
Supporting with facts
Supporting with quotations
Questioning stereotypes
Stating your message

Similarities	Differences
1. Both use emotive images of war and fighting. For example...	

5. There are various kinds of *media* which campaigners might use to get their message across. Discuss how each of the media listed in the box might affect what you have to say:

Letter to a newspaper
Speech at a meeting
Leaflet
Newspaper article
Car sticker
T-shirt
Banner
Poster

Case study: Local campaign

In this case study you will take part in a campaign to persuade a group of people to support your cause. See Techniques on p.173.

1. Selecting your role

Read the descriptions below of the roles of the Protesters and the Developers. Then as a class, choose who is to support each side. There should be more or less equal numbers on each side.

Protesters

As members of the Holt Protest Group, you are responsible for designing publicity to help persuade local people that a vast new housing estate will be a bad thing.

Developers

You are members of the team employed by Green Lands to persuade the people of Holt that the Peacock Farm development will be a good thing.

2. Designing the materials

Working in groups, each of you will produce *one* item of publicity material from the list on the right to support your side's point of view. Check that, as a group, you produce at least *one* piece of publicity from each of the three categories. The publicity your group designs will be on display at the public meeting (see page 172).

See *Ways of working* (p.176 onwards), for advice on how to prepare and present your publicity material. For each piece of work, prepare:

Written material
– a rough draft,
– a final version, typed or word-processed,
– photocopies if appropriate.

Visual material
– sketches of two or more designs (group to select),
– a 'mock-up' of the chosen design, e.g. of the poster, banner, hat,
– photocopies, if appropriate.

Audio-visual material
– a script,
– a tape/video recording.

Written

Newspaper article
Letter to a newspaper
Newsletter to local people
Leaflet or hand-out

Visual

Banner
Poster
Items to wear
Car sticker

Audio-visual

Radio commercial
Local TV interview

3. Holding a meeting

Hold a public meeting at which equal numbers of protesters and developers make their views known. This may be conducted either as one large meeting, or as two smaller ones, depending on the size of your class. While one half acts out the meeting, the other half could be a 'jury' and vote on which side puts up the more convincing case. Publicise your side's cause at the meeting by using your work from the case study. This can be done by:

- exhibiting poster lay-outs on the walls;
- 'selling' hats, badges, car stickers or other items;
- displaying banners carrying your own slogan;
- offering hand-outs and leaflets.

a) Choose to play the role of a person within the community who has a particular opinion to voice, using the list on the right as a guide. (Make sure that a wide range of roles is represented by your class.)

b) Work out what you will say at the meeting from your chosen person's point of view. You will be expected to introduce yourself, then talk for a minute or two, so make sure you have several things to say. Remember that you can also comment on what other people have said.

c) Appoint a strong chairperson who will invite each person at the meeting to speak in turn. S/he is responsible for making sure that no speaker is interrupted.

d) When each person has had an opportunity to speak, the chairperson can open the meeting to general discussion. This will give you a chance to ask other people questions, and to comment on any issues raised.

Shop-keeper
Member of an environmental group
Doctor/dentist
Unemployed person
Religious leader
School pupil
(Head)teacher
Parent
Commuter
Taxi driver
Housewife
Community leader
Builder
Old aged pensioner
Dog walker
Farmer
Estate agent
YTS trainee

TECHNIQUES

Campaigning

When you design your own campaign publicity, ensure that it is going to influence the way people think. To guide you, ask these five questions:

1. Who?

Who is campaigning? People reading your publicity must be clear whose side you are on. Possible ways to show this are to:

Logo
Name
Slogan

2. Says what?

What is the message of your publicity? Whether you are designing a poster with a short message or writing a newsletter with a longer message, aim to:

- arouse immediate interest, e.g. by being relevant to people's lives;
- indicate what your side is campaigning about;
- stir people's feelings, e.g. by using shock tactics;
- give important information.

3. To whom?

At whom are you aiming your publicity? Make sure that it addresses the right people – that is, your *target audience*.

This does not mean that you need write 'To all local people!' on the top of a poster. It might be more subtle to use:

- context: identify a place to put your poster where it will be seen by local people, e.g. your public library.
- message: choose words and images which strike people's attention and are clearly relevant to them, e.g. a picture of a bulldozer ploughing up a field.

4. How?
How are you going to get your message across? Your publicity will reach the target audience only if it uses the right medium. For example, if you want your local MP to hear your message, don't put a poster up in a sweet shop. Aim to:

5. With what effect?
How do you want the people reading your publicity to respond? You may want them to:

- **take notice:** think about an issue, perhaps for the first time;
- **reconsider:** feel shocked or disturbed enough to reconsider a fixed opinion;
- **take action:** send money, attend a meeting, join a campaign group.

- select a medium appropriate for the people you intend to persuade, e.g. a letter to an MP;
- select different media for different purposes, e.g. posters to make people more aware of an issue; newsletter to give specific information.

- Discuss how the Protesters and Developers might have applied these five questions to designing the newsletter on p.166, and the newspaper article on pp.168-169.

  WHO?
  How do the Protesters make clear who they are in the newsletter?
  How do the Developers make clear who they are in the article?

  SAYS WHAT?
  Find *one* sentence from both the newsletter and the article which summarises the message of each side.

  TO WHOM?
  How does the newsletter and the article each identify its target audience?

  HOW?
  Suppose that the Protesters had stated their case in a newspaper article, and the Developers had used a newsletter. Do you think this would have helped or hindered the case of either side?

  WITH WHAT EFFECT?
  What is the intended effect of the newsletter and the article?

Part Two

WAYS OF WORKING

KEEPING A STUDY LOG

A useful way of recording your thoughts and feelings about the texts you read and the work you do in English is to keep a study log. It may help you to generate ideas both for oral and written work.

The log may be something you write purely for yourself. Occasionally you may wish to show some part of it to a friend or to your English teacher.

In the log, write as freely as you want. You may wish to:

Record: Set the scene by describing briefly the work you are doing and how you are doing it (see log extract below). If you choose to summarise a text, make this short.

Question: Ask yourself questions about ideas, language, characters or events in the texts you read. Later on, you may resolve some of these questions and be able to record your findings.

Reminisce: Describe experiences and memories of your own, which have been stimulated by your English work.

Compare: Make comparisons between the texts you are reading and other texts you have studied.

Reflect: Think about the ideas, themes, thoughts and feelings expressed in the texts you read. Give your reactions and explain your own views.

Comment: Look at the style and expression of texts you study and comment on words, phrases, images and lay-out which make an impression on you.

Assess: At various points in your log, try to assess your own strengths and weaknesses in English – what you have achieved, what you find difficult, what kind of help you feel you need to overcome weaknesses.

> Date: 1st February 1999
> Subject: Describing People
> Text studied: 'The Welcome Table' by Alice Walker
>
> We read this short story in groups today, and then discussed it together. At first our group disagreed about the story's meaning. Does the old woman really meet Jesus on the high road, or is it a hallucination?

You will need either a separate exercise book or a separate section in a file to record your log. Distinguish each new entry from the previous one by starting a new page or by ruling a line. A page in your log might begin like the example on the left:

READING AND RESPONDING

If you are to respond to various kinds of writing, you should aim to be an active and critical reader. The study log (see p.176), is an excellent means of helping you both to understand and to question pieces of literature. The following techniques will help you with *other* types of writing – articles, adverts, manuals, leaflets, and so on.

1. Skimming

The aim of skimming (or *skim-reading*) is to get a quick, general impression of a whole piece of writing, without seeking to understand it in detail. This will help you to answer five central questions:

> **What** kind of text is it?
> **Who** has written it?
> **For whom** is it written?
> **What** is its basic message?
> **Why** was it written?

You can skim-read an article, a leaflet or an essay like this:

- Read the title.
- Read any large print – headlines, headings, slogans.
- Read the first sentence of each main paragraph.
- If the first and last paragraphs are short, read these quickly.
- Glance at any accompanying tables, diagrams or pictures.

Skim-read *Tainted Love* (see p.178) using the ways suggested, then answer the five questions above.

2. Scanning

Scanning or *scan-reading* is for more detailed reading, when you are searching for particular pieces of information. You may be asked to find a particular fact, a quotation or an answer to a question. Scan a piece of writing for information like this:

- Aim to speed up your reading. This will help you to concentrate on the information you are looking for.
- Read the first sentence of each paragraph again. This may announce the main topic for the rest of the paragraph, or at least help you to judge whether the paragraph is relevant or not.
- Have key words in your mind and look for those words as you read.

Scan *Tainted Love* for the following information:

> – Which countries have the higher car accident rate – rich or poor?
> – Find two examples of poor countries who spend a lot on cars.

3. Finding a pattern

All pieces of writing have an underlying pattern. If you can identify this, it will help you to summarise a difficult piece, to answer questions, and to use material from it for your own purposes. Find the pattern in this way:

- Divide the article below into sections – that is, find the start and finish of each new main point. Your sections will not necessarily correspond with the paragraphs.
- Note down any key words from each section.
- Write a word or phrase for each section, summarising what it is about.
- Draw a diagram of the pattern you have worked out, noting the links between one section and the next.

Complete this diagram showing the underlying pattern of *Tainted Love*.

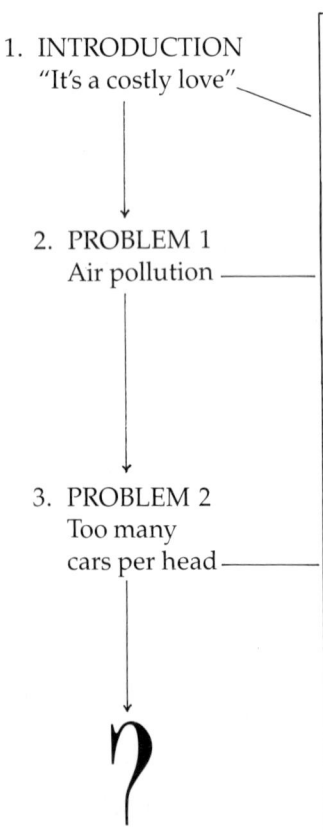

1. INTRODUCTION
"It's a costly love"

2. PROBLEM 1
Air pollution

3. PROBLEM 2
Too many cars per head

?

Tainted love
Motor mania

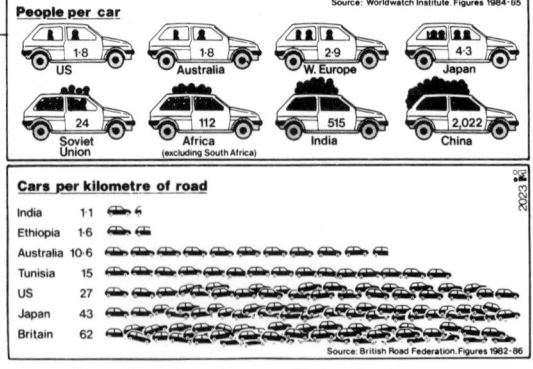

IT'S a costly love. And while the Western world is grappling – albeit somewhat feebly – with car addiction the Third World is increasingly falling under its spell. Thanks largely to private cars, São Paulo, Mexico City, Cairo and New Delhi have some of the worse air pollution problems in the world. In Calcutta 60 per cent of residents are believed to suffer from respiratory diseases related to air pollution.

Cities in rich countries do not do much better. Athens smog claims six lives a day. In the US the motor industry provides more than the great North American symbol of freedom and affluence. It also ensures that 75 million people live in areas that have substandard air. This is not surprising considering there is one car for every two people.

Chinese cities, by comparison, have one motor vehicle for every 2,000 people – and this is the example other developing countries should follow, says the Washington-based World Watch Institute in a recent study.

Quite apart from the effects on the environment – depleted oil reserves, air pollution, acid rain – car accidents claim more than 200,000 lives worldwide each year, with a sharp increase in developing countries. Safety standards are often inadequate. The report shows that in several Third World countries fatalities per mile can be 20 times higher than in industrialized countries and traffic accidents are now a leading cause of death.

The disproportionate amount of money and resources devoted to buying cars is also cause for concern. Haiti, the poorest country in the Western hemisphere, spends one third of its import budget on fuel, cars and car parts. Yet only one out of 200 people owns a car. Nigeria subsidizes fuel costs – despite its huge debt and the almost permanent traffic jam in the capital, Lagos. The resources of the poor and wealthy are drained, though only a few enjoy the benefits.

Rather than keep on importing cars Third World countries would do better to make use of their own rail systems, bicycles, rickshaws, pedicabs (motorcycle-drive rickshaws) pushcarts and tongas (animal-driven carts).

The chief lesson to be learned from the industrialized world's automobile addiction is an ironic one: by promoting the growth of sprawling cities with extensive suburbs the automobile has created more distance than it has overcome. To avoid falling into the same trap developing countries need to think more in terms of compact cities, with effective mass transit systems and affordable housing closer to where people work.

Elaine Shein/Gemini

People per car (Source: Worldwatch Institute. Figures 1984-85)
- US: 1.8
- Australia: 1.8
- W. Europe: 2.9
- Japan: 4.3
- Soviet Union: 24
- Africa (excluding South Africa): 112
- India: 515
- China: 2,022

Cars per kilometre of road (Source: British Road Federation. Figures 1982-86)
- India: 1.1
- Ethiopia: 1.6
- Australia: 10.6
- Tunisia: 15
- US: 27
- Japan: 43
- Britain: 62

THE WRITING PROCESS

There are several stages in almost any piece of writing:

- **Stage 1: Generating ideas**
- **Stage 2: Planning**
- **Stage 3: Drafting and redrafting**
- **Stage 4: Presenting.**

The following pages give you guidance on this process.

Where do ideas come from?

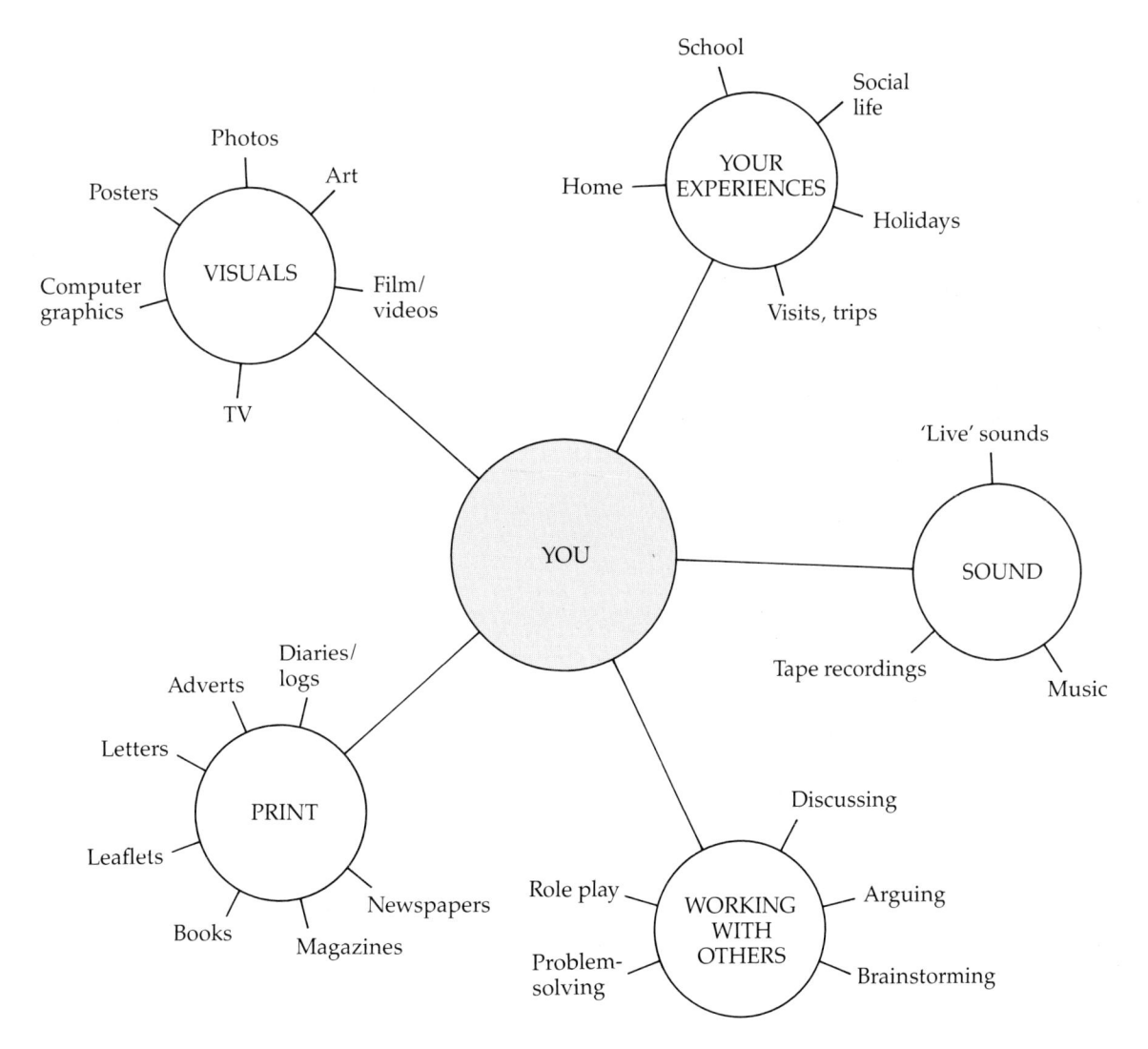

YOU

- **YOUR EXPERIENCES**: School, Social life, Home, Holidays, Visits, trips
- **VISUALS**: Photos, Posters, Art, Computer graphics, Film/videos, TV
- **SOUND**: 'Live' sounds, Tape recordings, Music
- **PRINT**: Diaries/logs, Adverts, Letters, Leaflets, Books, Magazines, Newspapers
- **WORKING WITH OTHERS**: Discussing, Role play, Arguing, Problem-solving, Brainstorming

Stage 1: Generating ideas

Many of the ideas for a piece of coursework will come from yourself, but it is often difficult to get started. Here are three methods:

1. Brainstorming

This means letting your mind 'think aloud', so that it generates a rapid number of ideas in a very short time. You should aim for a free flow of ideas associated with your topic, without judging how good or bad they are. It is the *quantity* of ideas, not the *quality* which is important in brainstorming.

Look at this example of brainstorming work by a group of students, carried out in four stages:

a) Write down all the words you associate with the topic of Fox Hunting.

fox	farmer	saboteurs
hounds	pest	heroes
horse	disease	activists
Tatler	chickens	radicals
bowler hats	shoot	anger
riding caps	guns	shout
tweed	pain	abuse
county	cruel	false trails
Meet	fear	police
sherry	scent	biased?
rich	rip	ruling class
snobby	tear apart	tradition
Pony Club	barbaric	heritage
squire	RSPCA	pleasure
manor		

b) Now put the words with something in common into groups.

1	2	3	4	5
fox	fox	tweed	heroes	police
pest	cruel	county	radicals	biased?
disease	hounds	Meet	saboteurs	RSPCA
chickens	scent	rich	activists	
shoot	tear apart	snobby	anger	
guns	barbaric	sherry	abuse	
farmers	fear	ruling class		
		squires		
		tradition		

c) Choose headings for each column:
   1. FOX: PEST
   2. FOX: VICTIM
   3. THE HUNTERS
   4. THE SABOTEURS
   5. OTHERS

d) Draw a plan which shows both the links between your ideas, and the conflicts or contrasts.

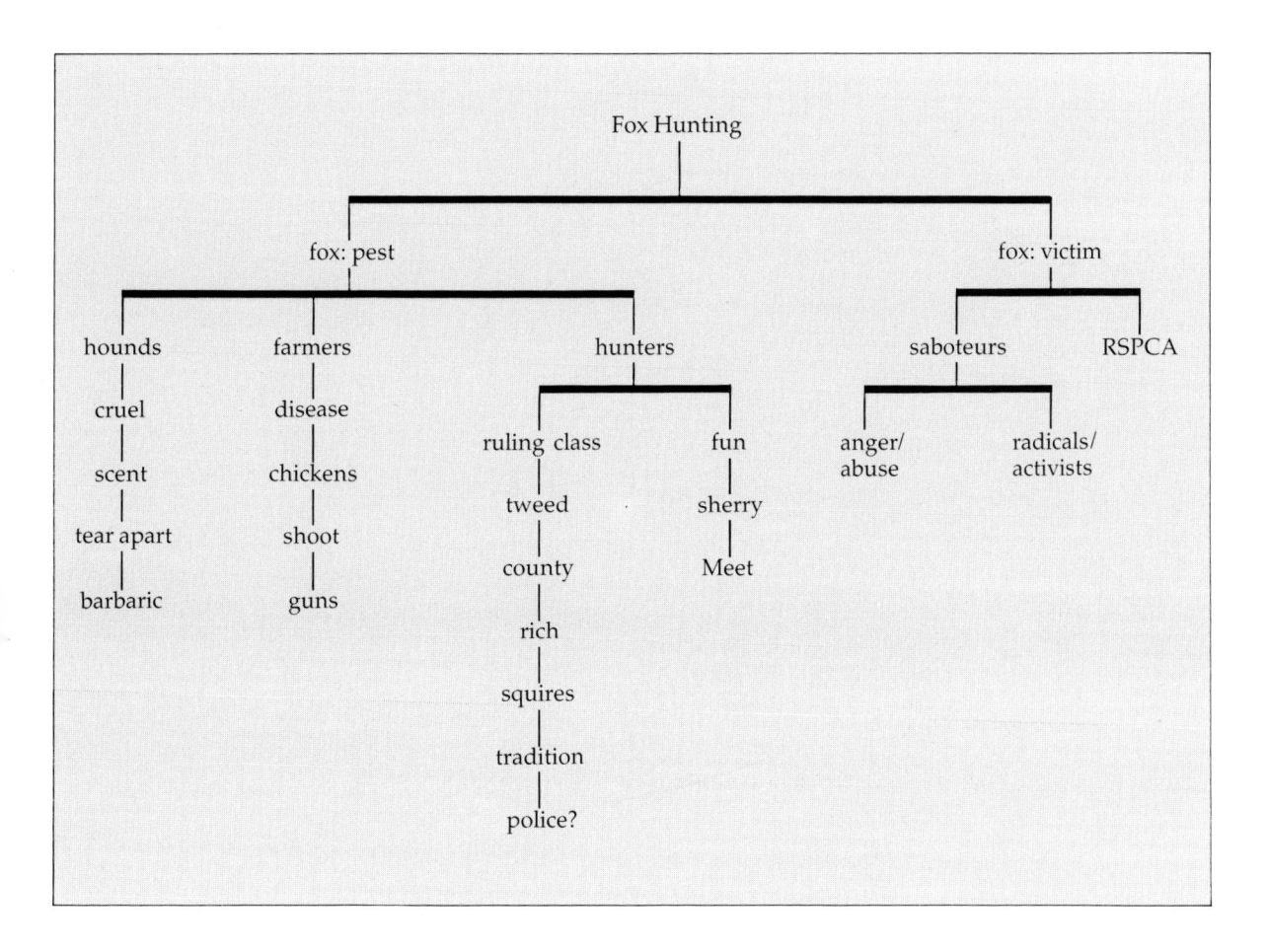

```
                              Fox Hunting
        ┌──────────────────────────┴──────────────────────┐
                    fox: pest                                   fox: victim
   ┌──────────┬──────────────┬──────────┐              ┌──────────┬──────────┐
 hounds     farmers         hunters                  saboteurs    RSPCA
   │          │         ┌──────┴──────┐              ┌────┴────┐
 cruel     disease   ruling class    fun          anger/     radicals/
   │          │          │            │           abuse      activists
 scent     chickens    tweed        sherry
   │          │          │            │
tear apart  shoot      county        Meet
   │          │          │
barbaric    guns        rich
                         │
                       squires
                         │
                      tradition
                         │
                       police?
```

> In groups or pairs, choose *one* of the following topics and follow the four stages of the brainstorming exercise:
>
> *smoking*   *football hooliganism*   *the future*
> *ghosts*   *space travel*

2. Using diagrams

Drawing a diagram may help you to develop and organise your thoughts – particularly when working on your own. Take a full page and write a short version of the topic in the centre. Then draw a line out from it and write the first idea you have on the topic. Draw other lines out from the centre for other main ideas. Look at this example on the topic:

Is school uniform a good idea?

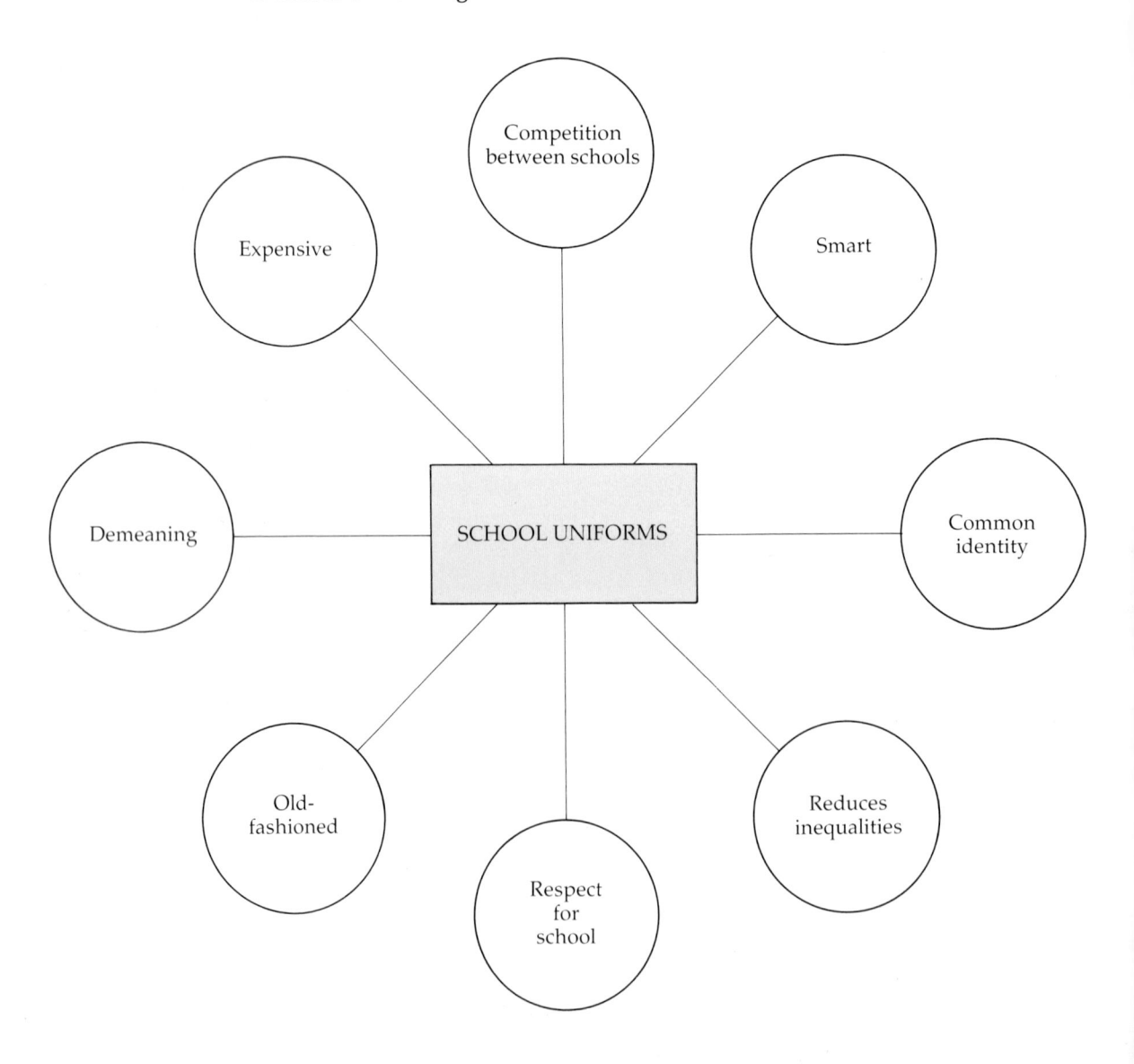

- Competition between schools
- Expensive
- Smart
- Demeaning
- SCHOOL UNIFORMS
- Common identity
- Old-fashioned
- Respect for school
- Reduces inequalities

Now add further ideas:

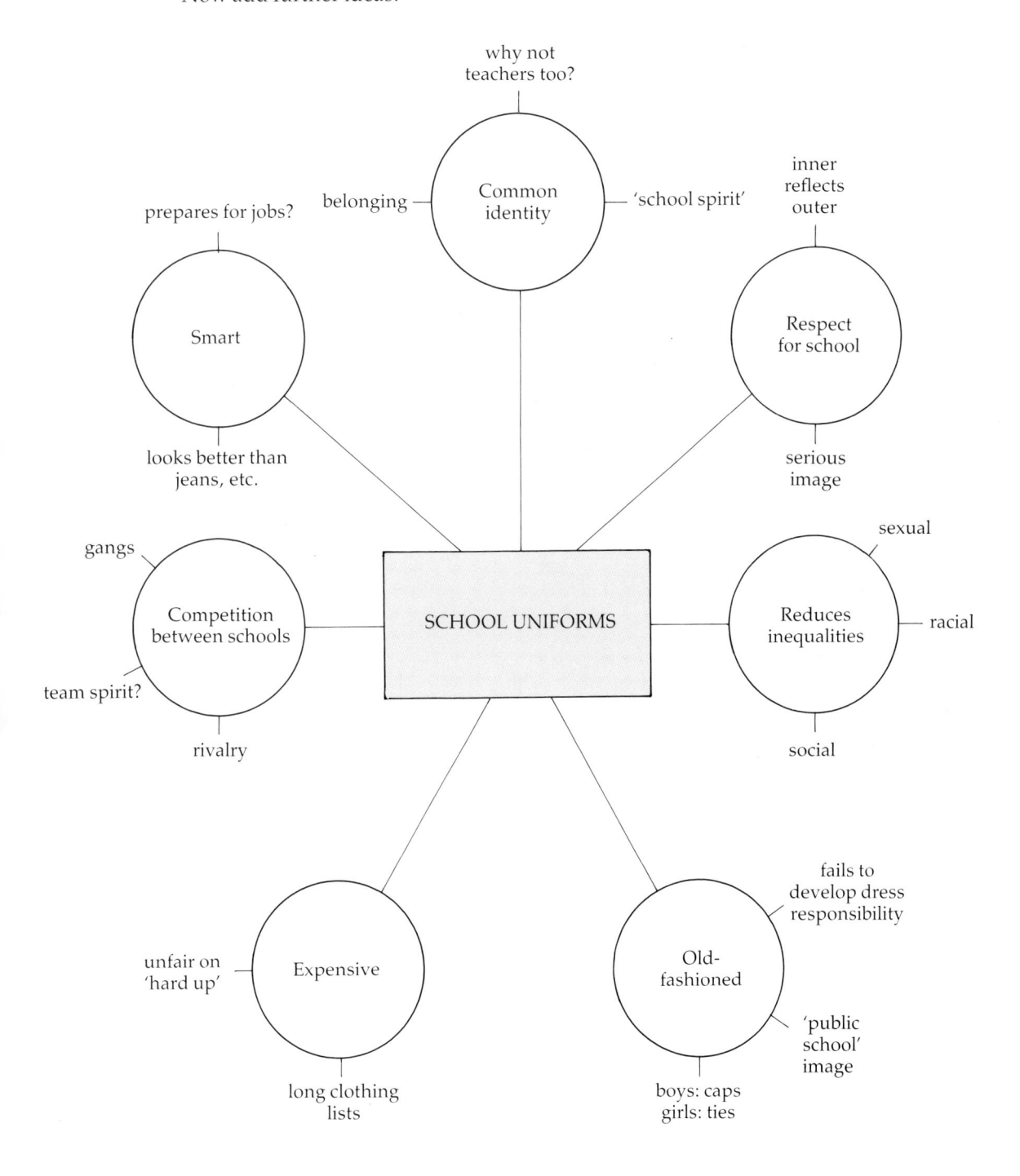

SCHOOL UNIFORMS (central topic)

- **Common identity**
  - why not teachers too?
  - belonging
  - 'school spirit'

- **Respect for school**
  - inner reflects outer
  - serious image

- **Smart**
  - prepares for jobs?
  - looks better than jeans, etc.

- **Competition between schools**
  - gangs
  - team spirit?
  - rivalry

- **Reduces inequalities**
  - sexual
  - racial
  - social

- **Expensive**
  - unfair on 'hard up'
  - long clothing lists

- **Old-fashioned**
  - fails to develop dress responsibility
  - 'public school' image
  - boys: caps, girls: ties

Draw a diagram like the one above for the topic:
Should school examinations be abolished?

3. Finding out

Once you have a skeletal framework of ideas, you may need to find out more information to check the opinions you have formed.

Various sources of information are available to you:

LIBRARY

subject catalogue reference books
notice-board telephone directories

OTHER PEOPLE

family class-mates teachers specialists
relatives friends

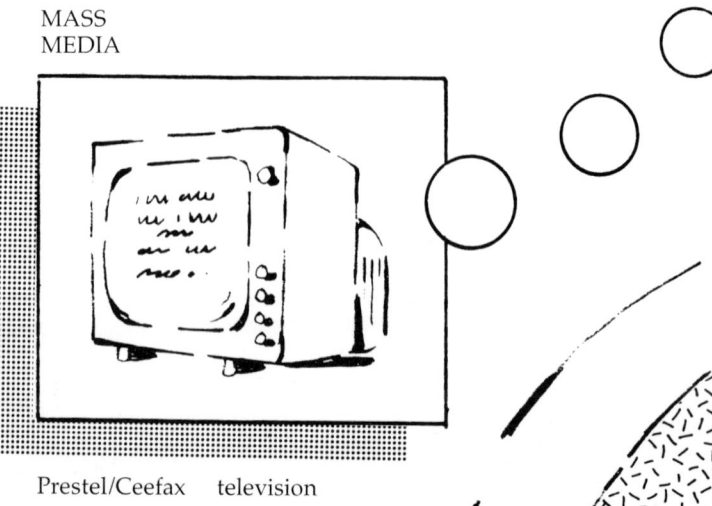

MASS MEDIA

Prestel/Ceefax television
newspapers radio magazines

PRESSURE GROUPS

RSPCA   Greenpeace   Shelter   YMCA

ADVICE CENTRES

Citizens' Advice   Samaritans   Helplines

Stage 2: Planning

The previous section suggested ways of generating and developing your ideas. The next stage is to make a plan to help you organise and present your ideas. The way you plan will depend on the nature of the work you have been assigned. There is no single, correct way to plan. Before you begin, think about the purpose of your work:

Audience: teacher, classmates, younger children?
Mode   : narrative, description, argument, mixture?
Form   : letter, interview, essay?

Your decisions will influence which type of plan you choose to make. Here are various models of plans:

Topic 1

Desert island

A popular approach to a topic like this is to tell a story. Another approach is to pick a *theme*. Suppose, for example, you have generated a large number of ideas which you have organised under these headings: ⟶

- The senses
- Contrasts
- Dawn to dusk
- Loneliness

Now select the theme which most appeals to you and note down which aspects of the theme could be used to structure your writing, like this: ⟶

1. Light/dark
2. Heat/cold
3. Beauty/savagery
4. Awake/asleep
5. Working/relaxing

You may wish to change the order, but you now have a basic shape to work with. Use the ideas you have previously generated to plan the content of each of the five paragraphs, like this:

Light/dark
Early morning: blue/grey, misty, opaque, everything blurred.
Mid-morning : stronger, yellow light; shadows forming, deepening.
Midday   : striking, stunning, bright light; black shadows.

Topic 2

Hand-out for a charity

When you are writing for a hand-out for a mass audience, it may be helpful to work through these two stages:

Organise what you have to say under section headings like those in the box, using graphs, tables and diagrams as well as written text.

> **STAGE 1:**
> Ask five questions
> **Who?**
> **Says what?**
> **How?**
> **To whom?**
> **With what effect?**
>
> **STAGE 2:**
> Identify section headings
> **Who we are**
> **The problems**
> **Our proposals**
> **How you can help**

Topic 3

Space exploration is a good thing

When you have gathered enough ideas and information, there are two useful ways of planning what you have to say:

The discussion approach:

FOR	AGAINST	CONCLUSION/ MY VIEW
1. One day the world may become over-crowded. We may need room to expand...	The human population is self-regulating. Wars, famines and other natural disasters control numbers...	I feel we *should* plan for the future of the human race. One option *is* space exploration...

The argument approach:

MY VIEW	WHY THIS IS RIGHT
1. Space exploration encourages nations to work together peacefully... 2.	Look at the Anglo-Soviet Juno mission...

OPPONENT'S VIEW	WHY THIS IS WRONG
1. There has always been competition between the 'super-powers' to own space...	This is a dated view. Recent events suggest that both sides wish to 'scale down' their 'Star Wars' technology...

Stage 3: Drafting and redrafting

Planning is one way of producing good writing. Another way, particularly in imaginative writing, is to make a rough draft. It is very difficult to have an idea and to write it down perfectly first time. That is why some professional writers prefer to get their thoughts on to paper quickly. Afterwards they can look back over what they have written, cross things out, alter words and sentences, and add new material. Other writers may make their first draft on a word-processor, with its facility to insert, delete and move text around. Whatever the drafting method, a piece of writing may be redrafted several times before a final version emerges.

Bernard Ashley has written a number of novels for teenagers. In *Janey*, he tells the story of a young girl's friendship with Nora, an independent old lady who has to go into hospital. The following pages show four stages in the process of writing a scene for the novel, from the first draft to the final, published version. In this scene, Nora is telling Janey and the hospital doctor how she intends to spend her future.

Have a look at all four versions in turn. Compare the handwritten draft with the final version from the novel. Discuss why you think Bernard Ashley has made the following alterations.

1. *The doctor looked up. She knew the law and all, Janey thought.*
   becomes
   The doctor looked up sharply. Janey pressed herself down on her seat.

2. *I will not be shunted off to Canada!*
   becomes
   I won't be shunted off somewhere like a sack of old potatoes, not to Canada or anywhere else!

3. *It suddenly came to Janey what she'd heard.*
   becomes
   Nora wanted to stay in her house!

4. *I'm staying right here in London where I belong!*
   becomes
   Not for the Queen of England am I moving out!

The first draft was written on every other line and on
every other page, to give room for redrafting:

INSERT "D" iii

"or I discharge myself from here... by you"

The doctor looked up. She knew the law and all, Janey thought.

"...And the second thing is... I'm staying in my own house. I will not be shunted off to Canada!"

It came to Janey suddenly what she'd said. She wanted to cheer.

"Not for anyone, I'm not moving out!"

But her throat had choked up. "You ain't... not.. going?" Janey managed.

"No, I ain't!" said Nora. And she smiled. "I'm staying right here in good old England, where I belong."

There was just nothing Janey could get out: not even a grunt to stand for all the delighted surprise she felt.

189

The second draft and first type-up, with redrafting:

"... So the first thing is, doctor, either I'm released by you or I discharge myself from here ..."

The doctor looked up. She knew the law, ~~and all~~ too, Janey thought.

"... And the second thing is ..." and here Nora took a very long drawn-in breath - "I'm staying in my own house. I will not be shunted off to Canada!" A metal trolley rattled past outside. Everywhere it still sounded normal, still ~~cheer.~~ It suddenly came to Janey what she'd heard. She wanted to stay just in her house! Nora says

"Not for anyone, I'm not moving out!" lumped with the rich news... ~~But her~~ Janey's throat had choked up, "You ain't ... not ... going?" she ~~Janey~~ managed. you're

The third draft and final type-up is now suitable for the publisher's and printer's use. Note that it was revised, just before submission.

"... So the first thing is, doctor, either you sign me off or I discharge myself from the ward..."

The doctor looked up sharply. Janey pressed herself down on her seat.

"... And the second thing is..." and here Nora took a long drawn-in breath..." if it's anyone's concern, I'm not budging out of my own house. I don't care what you say, I'm staying put. I won't be shunted off somewhere like a sack of old potatoes, not to Canada or anywhere else!"

A metal trolley rattled past outside, banged into a wall and made everyone look - otherwise Janey thought she'd have shouted, jumped, punched the air. Nora wanted to stay in her house! She rubbed the bruise on her arm which was suddenly tingling again. Was what she was hearing for real?

"Not for the Queen of England am I moving out!"

It was. And Janey's throat had choked up, was all lumped with the emotional news.

The fourth and final version, as it appears in *Janey*, is textually identical to the revised third draft – only the typeface differs.

> "...So the first thing is, doctor, either you sign me off or I discharge myself from the ward..."
>
> The doctor looked up sharply. Janey pressed herself down on her seat.
>
> "...And the second thing is..." and here Nora took a long drawn-in breath... "if it's anyone's concern, I'm not budging out of my own house. I don't care what you say, I'm staying put. I won't be shunted off somewhere like a sack of old potatoes, not to Canada or anywhere else!"
>
> A metal trolley rattled past outside, banged into a wall and made everyone look – otherwise Janey thought she'd have shouted, jumped, punched the air. *Nora wanted to stay in her house!* She rubbed the bruise on her arm which was suddenly tingling again. Was what she was hearing for real?
>
> "Not for the Queen of England am I moving out!"
>
> It was. And Janey's throat had choked up, was all lumped with the emotional news.

Drafting

Follow these guidelines when you write a first draft:

- Always use a rough notebook – for English work only, if possible.
- Write on one side of the page only and leave the opposite page blank. This will be used at the redrafting stage for noting down major alterations.
- Write on every other line, so that there is space to make minor alterations and corrections.
- Try to write your first draft rapidly. Don't worry about making mistakes or writing untidily. Like brainstorming, the idea is to put your thoughts and ideas down as soon as they occur to you, before you forget them. Don't judge what you have written until the redrafting stage.
- When you have finished, leave your draft for a while – a few hours at least. When you take a fresh look at what you have written, you will find it far easier to see ways of improving it.

Redrafting

Here is a checklist of questions to help you rethink, then improve what you have written.

> *Do you start your writing in a clear and powerful way?*
> *Will your reader be inspired to read on?*
>
> *How well have you organised what you have to say?*
> *Could the paragraph or sentence order be improved?*
>
> *Are there any sentences or words which add little to your writing?*
> *Should these be omitted?*
>
> *Are there any words or sentences which you should add, to give your writing better sense?*
>
> *Are there any words or expressions which could be rephrased to make a more powerful impact on the reader?*
> *Use a thesaurus or dictionary to help you.*
>
> *Is the ending strong? Is it relevant?*
> *The way you end a piece of writing will depend on its purpose.*
> *For example, does it clarify, summarise, provoke, surprise or shock?*

When you redraft a piece of writing:

- Do not rewrite the whole piece again at this stage. You can put a little star * or numbers at the place where you want to add something and then write it out on the opposite page or in the margin.
- Use a different coloured pen to make your alterations. This helps you to identify the alterations clearly when you write the second draft. Avoid using correcting fluid or rubbing out pencil corrections.
- Read your work out to a partner and ask him/her to comment, either generally, or on specific things like expression.
- If you have the opportunity, use a word-processor to draft, then redraft your work. This encourages you to be more experimental with redrafting and editing, because the whole process is usually less time-consuming!

Correcting

When you have written your second draft (and not before), consider how you can improve your technical use of English. Here is a checklist of questions to help you correct mistakes:

> *Have you spelt all the words you have used correctly? Use a dictionary to check any difficult words.*
>
> *Does any sentence sound clumsy when you read it aloud? Check with your teacher or a friend whether you have constructed it correctly.*
>
> *Have you indicated pauses in mid-sentence or at the end of a sentence by appropriate use of punctuation?*

When you correct your second draft, make sure you:

- Use a different coloured pen to make your corrections.
- Ask a partner to read your work through and comment on points of grammar, spelling and punctuation.

Stage 4: Presenting

Now write (or type) your final version.
Make sure you copy correctly from the second draft.
Concentrate on a neat and attractive presentation.

INTERVIEWING

This section looks at the skills you need to interview someone effectively. It is not about these skills you need when you are **being** interviewed, as these may depend on a particular situation. Being interviewed often requires playing a role in English work as it does in real life. See Role play on pp.197–198.

How to question

To be a good interviewer you need to know which type of question to ask. This will help you to find out what you wish to know about the person you are interviewing.

Suppose you are interviewing an older member of your family about their life history. If you want to encourage this person to talk freely, then ask the following question types:

1. Open-ended:	This allows the interviewee maximum freedom in answering.	
	e.g. *'Tell me about yourself...'*	
	'What are your feelings about...'	
2. Mirror:	This shows you are listening and understanding by mirroring the wording of an answer.	
	e.g. *'So, are you really saying that...'*	
	'In other words...'	
3. Hypothetical:	This enables the interviewee to think through a practical situation.	
	e.g. *'Suppose you were to do it this way...'*	
4. Prompting:	This helps the interviewee with a mental block or when s/he does not know how to answer the question.	
	e.g. *'How do you see your future...? Will you carry on with your work as a ... or will you retire soon?'*	

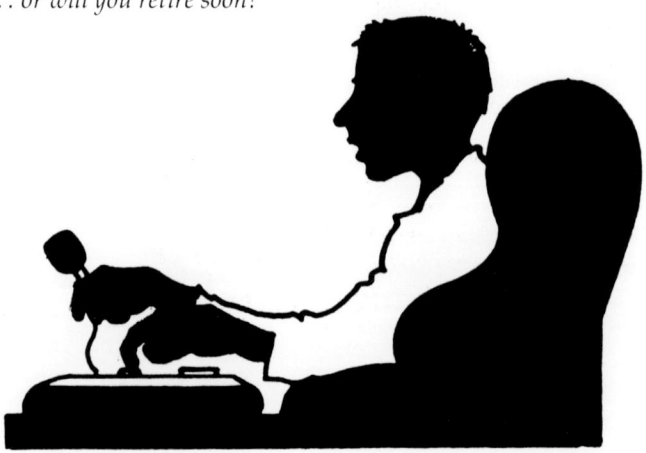

If the main purpose of the interview is to find out specific things, in, for example, a careers interview or a consumer survey, then the following question types may be more appropriate:

5. Close-ended: This allows interviewees little freedom in their response.
e.g. *'Which courses are you studying?'*

6. Yes/no: There are (more or less) two possible answers which again restricts the freedom of reply.
e.g. *'Do you like coursework assessment?'*

7. Loaded/leading: This makes it very obvious what the answer has to be.
e.g. *'Do you believe in all this nonsense about...?'*

8. Probing: This probes an interviewee's answer to get more information.
e.g. *'Could you give me an example of that point?'*

How to listen

An interviewer who is a good listener will encourage the interviewee to relax and speak freely. Most people like to be listened to, if only given the chance! You can show that you are a good listener in two ways:

Body language

Body language often indicates far more about your attitude to somebody than what you say. If you use the *right* body language, then you will encourage an interviewee to relax and develop answers fully. The *wrong* body language may be both threatening and off-putting.

	RIGHT	WRONG
Eye contact	Looking the interviewee in the eye. Occasionally glancing at your notes.	Staring continuously at the interviewee; *or* staring down at your notes, making no eye contact at all.
Facial expression	Looking interested by smiling and nodding your head.	Staring out of the window or around the room as s/he is talking. Looking bored or distracted.
Gestures	Making smooth, sweeping arm or hand movements when you ask a question.	Aggressive or restless movements such as finger jabbing, fidgeting, playing with a pencil, scratching or pulling your hair.

Spoken response

Your spoken response to what an interviewee has to say is also important. You have the power either to encourage them to speak further or to make them 'close off'. Here are some of the common ways of responding:

1. Encouraging

These are signs that you are listening and understanding.

e.g. *'I see...'*
'That's interesting...'
'Uh-huh.'

Examples of off-putting and discouraging remarks are:

'No... no, I don't agree at all...'
'Surely not...'

2. Restating

This is where you show a wish to understand by restating points.

e.g. *'So what you're saying is...'*
'In other words you think...'

There is a danger that you may have misinterpreted what the interviewee has said, but this response usually encourages clearer talk.

3. Reflecting

Here, you reflect the person's feelings and indicate some sympathy.

e.g. *'So you feel strongly that...'*
'You must have been very upset when...'

If you wanted to provoke the person, you might disagree with what they are saying by replying with 'loaded' questions or comments:

e.g. *'Surely you can't agree with the view that...'*

"...Aggressive or restless movements..."

ROLE PLAY

English work often asks you to imagine being someone else, or to imagine that you have feelings and attitudes which are different from your own. This is to help you to broaden your own experience of life, by understanding other people's views and experiences.

To be a good role-player, like a good actor, you have to 'get into' the skin and mind of the person you are playing. For some role plays, such as the interview of a 'personality', you may need to prepare a detailed character sketch, so all seven questions below will be useful. For other role plays, a more superficial character sketch might do. Use this checklist when you are preparing to role-play a character.

1. **What is their background?**
   - education;
   - job or career;
   - family life and personal relationships;
   - how poor or wealthy;
   - how successful or unsuccessful;
   - main interests in life?

2. **What are they like as people?**
   - reserved/confident;
   - humourless/witty;
   - rude/polite;
   - cold/warm-hearted?

3. **What events may have affected their lives?**
   - falling in love; marriage; divorce;
   - loss of someone close;
   - getting/losing a job;
   - public success or failure;
   - a physical addiction: to alcohol, etc.
   - an accident or illness?

4. **What attitudes and beliefs do they hold?**
   - towards other people: competitive or sharing;
   - towards themselves: how satisfied/dissatisfied;
   - towards politics, changes in our society etc;
   - towards religion: any particular faith?

5. **How do they speak?**
   - softly/loudly;
   - slowly/quickly;
   - shyly/confidently;
   - clearly/unclearly;
   - wittily/humourlessly;
   - which accent and dialect?

6. **How would they dress?**
   - formally/casually;
   - expensively/modestly;
   - fashionably/unfashionably;
   - smartly/untidily;
   - outrageously/conventionally?

7. **What body language is typical of them?**
   - gestures: typical arm/hand movements; quick/slow; relaxed/nervous; enthusiastic/bored?
   - expressions: how much eye contact; smiling/frowning; calm/restless; changing/constant;
   - posture: upright/slumped; relaxed/restless; dignified/ungainly?

Role-playing conventions

There are a number of useful conventions to help you structure your role play. These are:

Hot-seating

This involves placing one of you, or perhaps a group of you, in the 'hot seat', to answer questions posed by others in the class. If you are in the 'hot-seat', you may have a role as a criminal suspect, a character in a novel, or as a space pilot returned to earth for debriefing. If you are a questioner, you may be in the role of a detective, a barrister, a scientist, or a television interviewer.

The aim of *hot-seating* is to find out more about a character's personality and motives for behaving in a particular way.

Thought-tracking

This is where you have to imagine and express the inner thoughts of the character you are playing. For example, two people might play the same character, one speaking the outer dialogue, the other speaking the inner thoughts.

The aim of *thought-tracking* is to help you to understand a character's motives and behaviour more fully by comparing what is felt with what is actually said.

Still image

For this, a group of you will be asked to produce a 'tableau' which represents a particular moment, frozen in time. If you are asked to make a tableau of a memory (see p.9), aim to illustrate the nature of the event, the people involved and the relationships between them. You can do this by using gestures, facial expressions, posture and spaces between characters.

The aim of the *still image* is to help both the people participating and the people watching to appreciate the significance of a selected moment.

Role reversal

Role reversal is where you take the role of someone in your life, who may have a very different viewpoint or lifestyle from your own. For example, you may be asked to take the role of a teacher, doctor, person for whom you babysit, an employer, or a parent.

The point of *role reversal* is to put yourself inside the mind of someone else, in order to understand another, perhaps opposing, point of view.

FORMAL LETTERS

Formal letters are usually sent to people whom you do not know personally. For example, you would send a formal letter when:

- applying for a job
- making a complaint
- writing to a newspaper
- gathering information.

Lay-out

Use a *lay-out* like this, when writing a formal letter:

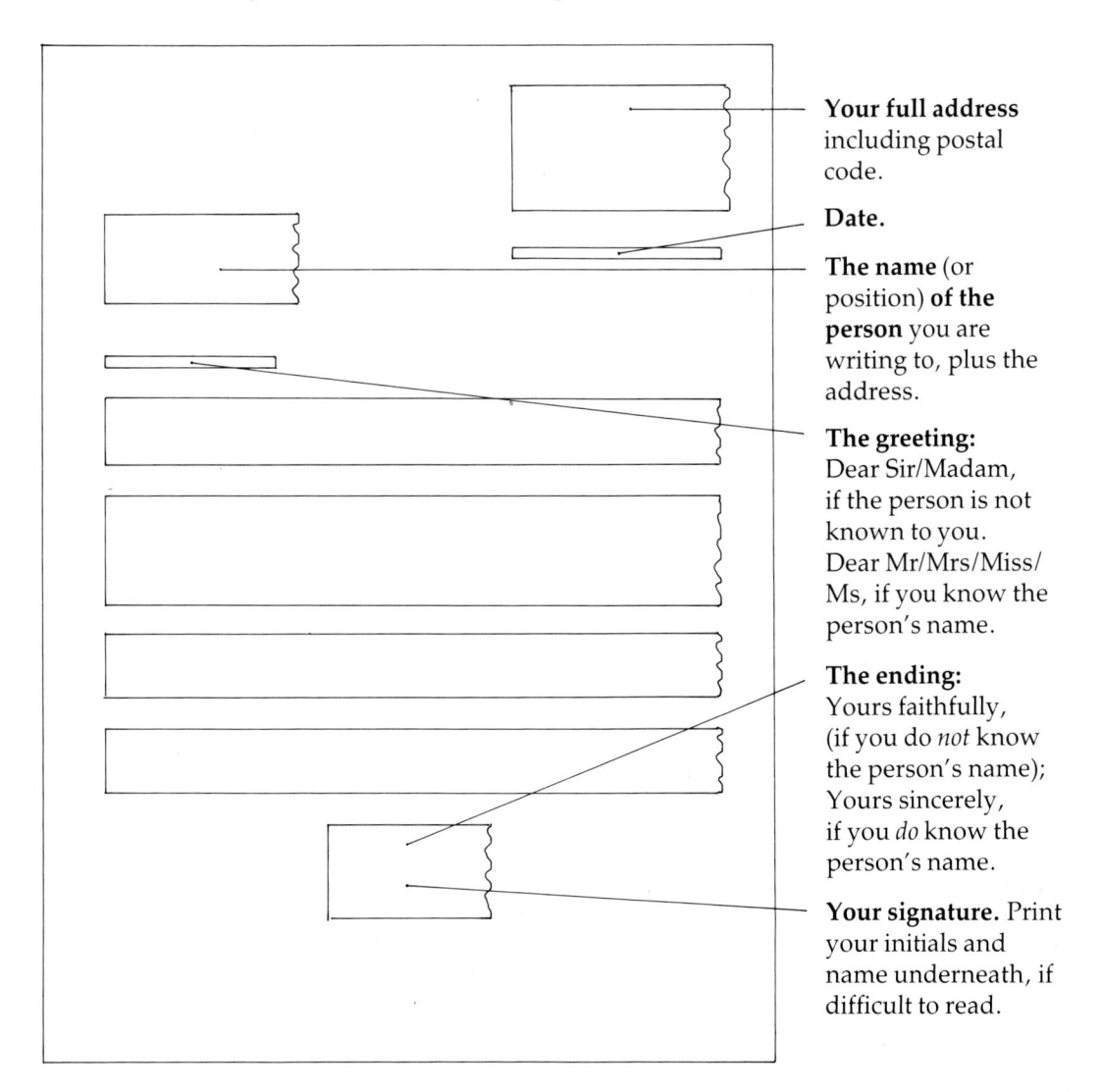

Your full address including postal code.

Date.

The name (or position) **of the person** you are writing to, plus the address.

The greeting:
Dear Sir/Madam, if the person is not known to you.
Dear Mr/Mrs/Miss/Ms, if you know the person's name.

The ending:
Yours faithfully, (if you do *not* know the person's name);
Yours sincerely, if you *do* know the person's name.

Your signature. Print your initials and name underneath, if difficult to read.

Content

Organise the *content* of your letter in this way:

The introduction

Use the first paragraph of your letter to summarise your reason for writing.

Main body of letter

Give a fuller account of your reason for writing the letter. Divide this into clear, concise paragraphs.

Conclusion

Summarise the main point of your letter and, if appropriate, say what you want to achieve.

> **Keep right on touting**
>
> SIR — Those people who are trying to reduce the profits of Wimbledon tennis ticket touts (report, Jan. 11) "in order to bring more profits to the sport" are making a big mistake.
>
> The touts do a great service to those lovers of the game who have been unlucky in the draw and are unable to stand in a long queue for hours. If people wish to spend money on such tickets, knowing the original price of the ticket, instead of on video recorders or things like that, of what concern is this to the Wimbledon authorities?
>
> Many people are selling properties at prices and profits well above the original or even real value of the property. Does anyone denounce them for taking these profits? Why should the touts be hounded for making a profit?
>
> Incidentally those fortunate enough to get a ticket from a tout are just as likely to spend money in the museum, refreshment areas and shops as those who queue to get in.
>
> I have depended on touts at Wimbledon for many years and I am grateful to them and hope they will be left to continue in peace.
>
> PATRICIA BARNARD
> Saffron Walden, Essex

from *The Telegraph*

Register

If you write a formal letter in an appropriate *register*, it will receive more consideration. Formal letters are usually written in Standard English (see p.66 for definitions). Patricia Barnard might have stood less chance of getting her letter published in *The Telegraph*, if she had used the same register as the one in the heading, for example:

> *What that report on ticket touts said last week is a load of old rubbish.*
> *Touts are real heroes; you can't stick all the blame on to them for the way the punters blow their readies. What about all those con artists selling their houses over the odds? No one's ticking them off for chancing their hand.*
> *Anyway, who's to say those of us with the savvy to buy from touts won't spend loads of money once we get in, just like the berks who queue?*
> *Just keep your hands off the touts. So what if they make a bob or two? I say keep right on touting!*

LEAFLETS

A leaflet is a basic part of any publicity campaign. It usually aims to persuade a mass audience to change its opinions and/or take a course of action, e.g. give a donation, become a member. The style and contents of each leaflet will depend on who is going to read it and what it has to say. Here are some general guidelines:

Appearance

The common feature of a leaflet is that it is a single, *folded* sheet of paper. But there are several variations of this theme. For example:

Title

Give your leaflet an eye-catching and informative title. Well chosen *puns* and words with double meanings can be effective.

e.g. *Raise the Roof* was the title of one of Shelter's campaigns. (A publicity sheet for this campaign is featured on p.146.)

The reader

Aim the text of your leaflet at a specific reader.

e.g. If you are writing for young people of a particular age, express your points in a way that this group will understand without feeling patronised. Also try to appeal to their interests and experience.

Content

Your leaflet should contain a mixture of *argument*, *evidence* and *proposals*. Support each main point of your argument with hard facts (such as statistical evidence). Proposals can only be made on the basis that a case has been argued convincingly.

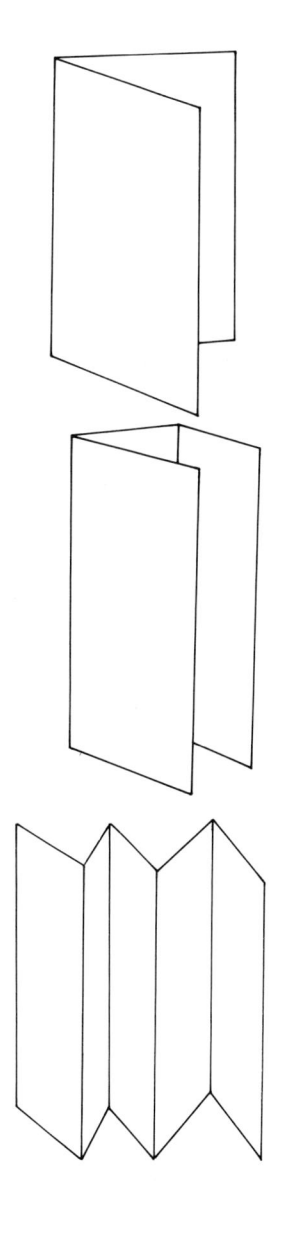

Structure

Organise the information inside your leaflet into clear sections which have a logical sense of direction and purpose. Use these guidelines:

Introduction: give:
the name of the campaigning group(s);
the name and point of the campaign;
the people at whom it is aimed.

Main information sections: give:
the reasons which make action necessary;
the campaign's solutions or policies.

Conclusion: summarise the main argument: propose what your readers can do to help the campaign – send money; become a member; take a vote; joint a protest; then finish with an eye-catching slogan!

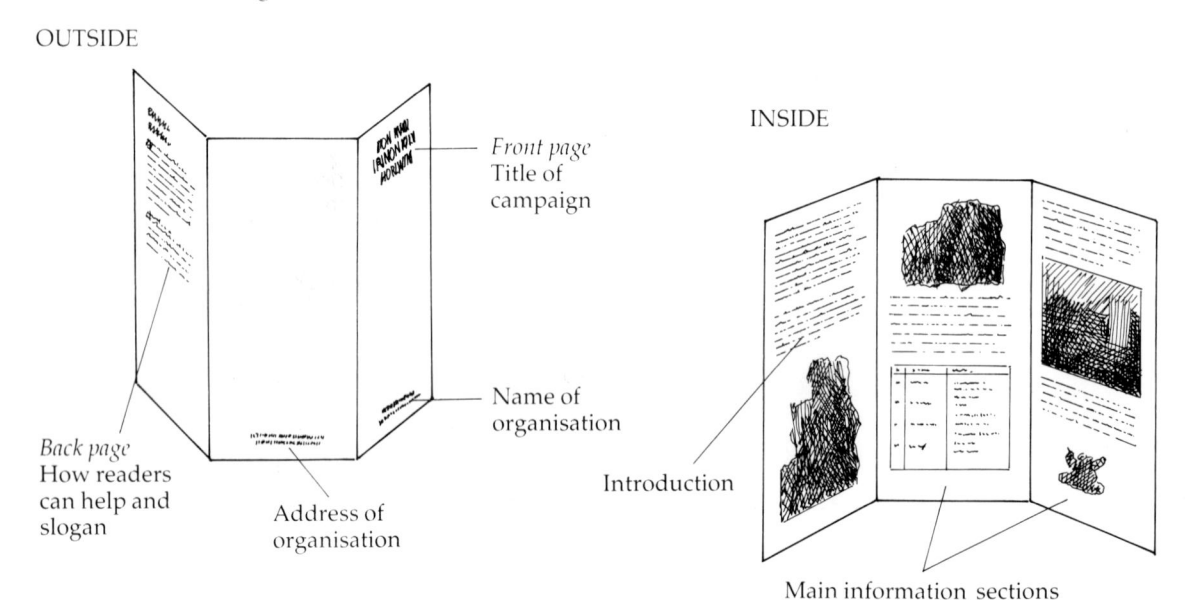

OUTSIDE

Front page
Title of campaign

Back page
How readers can help and slogan

Address of organisation

Name of organisation

INSIDE

Introduction

Main information sections

Presentation

Design your leaflet so that it can be read quickly. Make your points as clearly, simply and concisely as possible without distorting the main argument. Avoid long chunks of text!

Ensure that each heading and section is interesting to look at and easy to read. Variation can be introduced by using two or three colours; different print sizes; spacings; diagrams, charts and illustrations.

SOUND SCRIPTS

The case study activity on p.148 is used here to illustrate how to draft a sound script and a storyboard.

A sound script for a tape-slide sequence, or for a radio commercial, may combine any of the following elements:

Sound effects: any sound other than speech used to create a sense of 'background', such as music, footsteps, traffic, bird song, and so on.

Commentary : a 'voice-over' narrating or explaining the subject matter.

Dialogue : spoken by two or more of the people involved, often an interview or a conversation.

A typical lay-out for a script should look like this:

Subject: Teenage Homelessness *Title:* 'Susan Leaves Home'			
Slide no.	Duration	Sound effects	Commentary/dialogue
1	20 secs	Lively disco music.	Susan enjoyed life. She had many friends. She had a boyfriend she loved. She was looking forward to finding a job when the school term ended.
2	15 secs	Disco music fades.	But before long everything was to turn sour...

STORYBOARDS

A storyboard is a plan of what will be shown in each 'shot' of a film, slide sequence or television commercial. Also it may include directions for the actors, camera crew and lighting operators.
(See opposite for the coding of camera shots.)

After drafting your script, the next stage is to decide which images should illustrate it. Use a storyboard to plot the different scenes or events. Set this out rather like a strip cartoon on a large sheet of plain paper:

| LOCATION:
DURATION:
CAMERA SHOTS:
DESCRIPTION: | A disco with flashing lights, bright colours.
20 secs.
MCU to CU on Susan.
Susan enjoying herself with friends at a disco. | A teenage girl's bedroom at home; posters on wall.
15 secs.
PAN, MCU, CU.
Susan, crosslegged on bed, face in hands. | A city railway station.

20 secs.
PAN, ZI, MCU.
Susan, waiting for a train to arrive. Looks at purse. |

If you are not confident about outline drawing, then:

- ask a friend to help you;
- draw stick people;
- make written notes instead.

TELEVISION OR FILM SCRIPTS

Here are some working guidelines for producing a script for sound and camera:

1. Use a larger version of the form below to give directions for camera shots, and a description of what is on the sound track at any given time.
2. The sound track is likely to be mainly dialogue with some music and sound effects. Consider whether or not you will use a narrator as a 'voice-over', who may explain the links between scenes.
3. Use sketches (line drawings or stick people will do), or describe the picture in words, to show the subject of each visual frame – that is, what the camera is to film. Number each frame in sequence.
4. To show the camera movements required to capture each frame, use the standard coding:

Close-up	CU	(face or detail)
Fade-in	FI	
Fade-out	FO	
Long-shot	LS	(group or scene in total)
Medium close-up	MCU	(face and half body)
Pan	PAN	(swing camera around a scene)
Zoom in/Zoom out	ZI/ZO	

No.	VISUAL (Sketch or description)	CAMERA SHOT	SOUND (Music, dialogue, voice-over)

DIRECT SPEECH

Look at the use of direct speech in the epilogue (end piece) of Bernard Ashley's novel, *Janey*.

She bumped into Mary on her way home, rushing all important in her blazer for a seventy-five bus. "How's it goin', Mare?" *she asked.*

"All right, Janey. Got me gold! It's bein' engraved. How you going yourself?"

"Mustn't grumble. Worse troubles at sea."

She saw the old smile in Mary's eyes, the mates they'd used to be.

"Here, Mare, couldn't lend us two tens till tomorrow, could you?" *It was on the spur of the moment, but somehow thought out all the same.*

"I dunno." *Mary frowned, made a show of feeling in her pockets. Then she suddenly proved the smile had been genuine.* "Here y'are Janey, till tomorrow..." *But she didn't hand the coins over till Janey had told her some more.* "You ain't robbin' a bank tonight, then? That makes a change, don't it?"

"Yeah – given it up!" *Janey said, straight.* "Ringing the police instead."

"Stroll on!" *Mary laughed, no nearer to understanding the girl.*

She ran off to her gymnastics: while Janey went on where she'd just left off, forgetting her bruises for the leaps and springs of her mind, away up the street towards the twin telephone boxes, the pair that were never out of order. She didn't know what good it would do, or even if anyone would listen to some kid's voice putting the finger on the Catholic Club job. But of one thing she was certain: from now on Janey Pearce wasn't going to be fighting her battles on her own.

1. Use double "_____" or single '_____' inverted commas around each speaker's words.
2. If you put *she said*, (or similar), before the speech, put a comma before the inverted commas:
   She said, "All_____."
   Then start the speech with a capital letter.
3. If you put *she said* in the middle of a speech, follow these words with a comma or a full stop:
   "All_____," *she said,* "you_____."
   "All_____," *she said.* "You_____."
   Use a small letter after *she said*, and a capital letter after *she said*.
4. Every time there is a new speaker, start a new line/paragraph.

PLAY SCRIPTS

If the epilogue to *Janey* (see opposite) were to be written as a play script for actors, it could be set out like this:

> *(A row of suburban houses. As MARY rushes importantly for a no. 75 bus, her friend JANEY bumps into her.)*
>
> JANEY: How's it goin', Mare?
>
> MARY: All right, Janey. Got me gold. It's bein' engraved. How you going yourself?
>
> JANEY: Mustn't grumble. Worse troubles at sea. *(JANEY notices MARY'S friendly expression. Then, quickly but deliberately.)* Here, Mare, couldn't lend us two tens until tomorrow, could you?
>
> MARY: *(at first frowns and makes a show of feeling in her pockets, then suddenly proves the smile is genuine.)* Here y'are, Janey, till tomorrow...
> *(MARY still doesn't hand over the coins, as if waiting for JANEY to tell her some more.)* You ain't robbing a bank tonight, then? That makes a change, don't it?
>
> JANEY: *(straight.)* Yeah – given it up! Ringing the police instead.
>
> MARY: *(laughing but looking perplexed.)* Stroll on! *(MARY runs off to her gymnastics: while JANEY carries on as she left off, walking with determination towards twin telephone boxes.)*

1. Print in CAPITAL LETTERS: the names of speakers and of any characters named in the stage directions.
2. Set out the names of speakers directly underneath each other.
3. Do not put quotation marks around speeches.
4. Leave a blank line between each new speaker.
5. Setting descriptions appear at the beginning of each scene and describe location, time and mood. Put these in brackets.
6. Stage directions describe actions and behaviour, such as entrances and exits, body language and style of speech. Put these in brackets. Setting and stage directions are usually printed in *italic* type.

DESIGNING A POSTER

A poster is designed to be seen from a distance by people who are on the move. It should create an immediate impact by communicating its message in a concise and forceful way. However, a poster will be of little value if it does not make sense. When you design a poster of your own, check that it answers the five Q's below:

Says what?

A SOBERING THOUGHT.

THINK YOU CAN DRINK AND DRIVE? THINK AGAIN.

Who?   To whom?   Says what?   With what effect?   Who?

WHO? A well-known organisation may simply use a logo, with its name in the small print. If less-known, make your name clear.

SAYS WHAT? Use a short, forceful and memorable slogan, summarising your message.

TO WHOM? You can indicate your target audience by your use of words and pictures, as well as by *context* – for example, a drink-drive poster outside a pub.

HOW? With words: play on double meanings using *puns*.
With pictures: use striking images which surprise, amuse or shock.

WITH WHAT EFFECT? Indicate how you want your target audience to respond to the poster – think again? Send money? Contact an address? Buy something?

208